How to Live with Your Kids

When You've Already Lost Your Mind

Other Books by Ken Davis

How to Live With Your Parents
Without Losing Your Mind
I Don't Remember Dropping the Skunk
But I Do Remember Trying to Breathe:
Survival Skills for Teenagers
Secrets of Dynamic Communication:
Preparing and Delivering Powerful Speeches

How to Live with Your Kids

When You've Already Lost Your Mind

Ken Davis

ZondervanPublishingHouse

Grand Rapids, Michigan

A Division of HarperCollinsPublishers

How to Live With Your Kids When You've Already Lost Your Mind
Copyright © 1992 by Ken Davis

Requests for information should be addressed to:
Zondervan Publishing House
Grand Rapids, Michigan 49530

Library of Congress Cataloging-in-Publication Data

Davis, Ken, 1946–
   How to live with your kids when you've already lost your mind /
Ken Davis.
     p. cm.
   ISBN 0-310-57630-X (hardcover)
   1. Parent and teenager. 2. Parenting—Religious aspects—
Christianity. I. Title.
[HQ799.15.D38 1992
649′.1—dc20
                                         92-8396
                                            CIP

All Scripture quotations, unless otherwise noted, are taken from the HOLY BIBLE: NEW INTERNATIONAL VERSION® (North American Edition). Copyright © 1973, 1978, 1984, by the International Bible Society. Used by permission of Zondervan Publishing House.

"NIV" and "New International Version" are registered in the United States Patent and Trademark Office by the International Bible Society.

Edited by Dave Lambert
Cover design by Dennis Hill

Printed in the United States of America

92 93 94 95 96 97 / DH / 10 9 8 7 6 5 4 3 2 1

CONTENTS

INTRODUCTION

I had just finished speaking to several thousand teenagers when a sad-faced girl came up to the stage and said, "Oh, Mr. Davis—I wish you were *my* dad." I was about to pat myself on the back when I heard an odd noise and turned around. Behind me, my oldest daughter was responding to the girl's statement by sticking her finger down her throat and making gagging noises.

Even that daughter will vouch for my basic character, but she and the other members of my family will quickly tell you that I am not the perfect parent. Nor am I a famous psychologist, a movie star, or even a successful criminal. So why should I write this book?

First, because so many parents have asked me to. As I have conducted parent-teen seminars across the country, I have often referred to my first family book, *How to Live With Your Parents Without Losing Your Mind.* Over and over again, moms and dads at those seminars asked me to consider writing something for parents who had *already* lost their minds. At first, I was reluctant—I don't consider myself an expert on parenting.

But as the requests continued, I remembered that some of the most valuable help and encouragement I have received as a parent came as I sat around a kitchen table drinking coffee with friends who also had children. Those conversations showed me the practical application of the information gained from hundreds of books and dozens of seminars. Here were people who were actually *living* with kids. (Or should I say, people who had kids and were actually still living.) Here were people who had tried what they had heard or read, kept the stuff that worked, and trashed what didn't; people who were experiencing firsthand the heartaches and joys of parenthood; people who cared how things were going in my family because they knew exactly what we were going through. I always left those sessions encouraged that I was not alone, excited about the things I was doing right, and determined to change the things I was doing wrong.

I would like this book to work for you in exactly the same way. I would like you to feel, when you've read it, that you've been sitting down over coffee with a friend and fellow parent.

Although I'm not an expert, neither am I totally without qualifications. And I'm not ashamed to place high on that list the fact that I'm a parent of two teenagers and that I care deeply about the struggles that you and I face as parents.

I offer as additional qualification a life of unique experience with kids and their parents. Over the past twenty years, I have spent thousands of hours with thousands of kids and parents. I have spoken to over one million high-school and junior-high students across the U.S. and in other countries. My heart has been broken as I've talked with kids who felt no one cared, and broken again when I met parents (sometimes of those same kids) who didn't know how to show that they cared. I've spoken to thirteen-year-old boys in detention centers and wealthy suburban kids living in another kind of prison of their own making. My personal study of parenting, the years of reacting with parents and teenagers, and the reality of being a bona fide parent (lost mind and all) has taught me some principles that have been tremendously helpful. I still have much to learn, of course—but if I had waited until I learned it all to write this book, your kids would have been grown before it was completed.

As I write, I can look up from my desk at a library of books written by the experts. There's a wealth of information on those shelves that I hope is synthesized here. I pray that the ideas gained from those years of experience and study will come together in this book in the form of practical steps that you and I can use to improve our performance as parents, starting today.

Are you a single parent? Let me encourage you; even though many of the discussions in this book seem to refer to the "traditional" American family, these principles will work just as well for you. Please don't let the often-traditionalist language of the book make you think you've been left out—you were in my mind with every chapter. My hat is off to the wonderful parents I see doing a difficult but possible job alone, using every bit of their creativity and energy to give their kids a life of love and security. I pray that you will be encouraged and your load lightened by what you find on these pages.

One other caution: Good parenting does not guarantee happy and productive children. I hope you'll be challenged to be the best parent you can possibly be—and that you'll be able to trust God to do the rest. If your heart is broken because of a difficult or wayward child, don't add to that sorrow by blaming yourself. Allow God to help you make the changes you need to make in your life, and trust that he will be working in the life of your child as well. Ironically, your success as a parent is not best measured by the changes in your children, but rather by the changes in you.

This book was almost not written—or perhaps I should say, was written twice. Two months before the deadline for the submission of my manuscript, the hard disk on my computer crashed, destroying a year's worth of work. From the stress and (let's be honest) the agony, my body immediately broke out in red welts. But the very next day, I found a hard copy of my first draft and began to work again in earnest. Two-and-a-half hours later, the maid came into the hotel room and kicked out the power plug—destroying, of course, all the work I'd entered into my computer in the meantime. I tried, momentarily, to set aside my own feelings to comfort the distraught maid. (She had never seen a grown man cry before.) Several hours later, when I had retyped most of what I had lost that morning, lightning struck and the power went out. It was gone again. This time my screams probably frightened the entire county.

The fact that I still have my sanity, the maid is still living, and this book was finished may be evidence of a miracle. I hope that will be *your* conclusion as you read the book.

1

I'm Not Okay, You're Not Okay, But That's Okay

Being Abnormal Is Normal

I never wanted to be a parent. It isn't that I hated kids—
it's just that one night I was unfortunate enough to meet
one.

My wife, Diane, and I were invited to dinner with people we
had thought were our friends, and I found myself seated next
to a small child armed with food and sharp utensils. That night
I was the target for a veritable artillery barrage of reconstituted
baby cuisine. Since I have a weak stomach to begin with, it's
my view that once food has entered the mouth, it should never
be seen again. During the entire evening, I never saw *any* food
stay in this baby's mouth. Most of it never *reached* the mouth.
Any food that wasn't smeared over some part of his body was
catapulted toward me.

To this day, I'm convinced that toddlers don't have stom-
achs. They receive nourishment by absorbing food through
their pores. What food *does* enter the mouth is met by a
rejection system that immediately returns it so that it can be
smeared on the body and absorbed. This child smashed an
entire bowl of peas and hid them in his left ear. When the
mother exclaimed, "Isn't that cute!" my own food rejection
system was almost activated.

"I don't want to have any children," I confessed on the way home that evening.

"Thank you," my wife whispered, rubbing at the stains of smashed peas and jello on her new dress.

But on our next trip to see the doctor, he told us that we didn't have to worry about it—children were out of the question. It was physically impossible for us to have kids, he said. We now have a sixteen-year-old daughter we named Physically, and a thirteen-year-old daughter who is Impossible—and a different doctor. Miraculously, our children are very well adjusted. I wish I could say the same thing about their parents.

There's no way to fully prepare for the cultural shock of having children. When we found out we were going to be parents, we attended every parenting class within a 500-mile radius. Those classes, unfortunately, are like playing the stock market with mock investments—it's *nothing* like the emotional roller coaster of using your own money. Likewise, trying to analyze what you will do when you have your own children is nothing like the surprise that awaits you when they actually arrive.

After the classes, I was convinced that I was capable of effectively parenting any kind of child my wife was capable of bearing. Well, I grossly overestimated my parenting skills and totally underestimated the kind of child my wife was capable of bearing. Two months into real parenthood, I flushed the contents of our aquarium, convinced that I wasn't even capable of caring for fish.

But maybe that wasn't such a bad beginning; from that position of confessed inadequacy, I began to learn to be a better parent. I still don't have all the answers—in fact, anyone who claims to have all the answers doesn't have children. As a father who has made a lot of mistakes but wants to be a better parent, as a former youth worker who's been immersed in the teenage subculture most of my life, I think I have some insights that will help you see parenting from a different perspective. You may even learn to laugh at yourself—an ability that can give you the courage to allow God to help you make some important changes.

Over the years, I've been privileged to research and write two books about parents and their children. It's my prayer that the result of that research, coupled with the information and insight gleaned from hundreds of face-to-face meetings with parents and their children at family seminars, will both encourage you and give you practical help in coping with parenthood.

In this chapter, I'd like to explain three principles that can help you be a better parent and enjoy it more. First: No parent is perfect—but that's okay, because perfection is not a requirement for parenthood. Second: Confession is good for your own soul and essential for the well-being of your children. And third: Effective parenting is measured not by the changes you force in your children but by the changes you allow God to make in you.

You're Not Okay, But That's Okay

When we found out that Diane was pregnant with our first child, Traci, there was none of the usual jubilation that accompanies the news of impending parenthood. Right up to the moment of birth, I was ambivalent (if not downright angry) about this intrusion into our lives. I'm surprised Diane didn't leave me during those nine months.

My attitude was terrible. I nearly got kicked out of Lamaze class when, after they'd showed the birthing movie, I yelled, "Run it backwards!" (The leader didn't have much of a sense of humor.)

Despite that lousy attitude, I brought two cameras to the delivery room—but I have no pictures. After all those months of ambivalence, when Traci actually entered the world I was so overwhelmed with love that I just sat in a corner and wept.

The turbulent, surprising emotions I felt that day hid another change that began at the same time: The brain cells that rule over common sense had begun to die. I was becoming a bona fide parent. And the effects were immediate. As the doctor held up what looked like a beautiful little red-headed prune, I ran from the room to call my wife to let her

know. I made it to the hall before I realized that she probably wasn't home.

The downward spiral continued. Within weeks, I was cheering Traci's efforts to fill a diaper. Before long, I found myself saying, "Isn't that cute!" as she smashed peas and hid them in her ear.

Diane, too, was severely affected. "If you poke your eyes out with those scissors, don't come looking for me," I heard her yell one afternoon. Another day she exclaimed, "Look at me when I'm talking to you!"—immediately followed by, "Don't you look at me like that!"

Hope for recovery was all but gone by the time Traci reached childhood; I realized that when I trapped her in a corner one evening and began shaking my finger in her face. When I was a boy, my father would do the same thing to me, and it drove me nuts. "What's wrong with you?" he would demand, wagging his finger just inches from my nose. I wanted to shout, "Your finger!" But my desire to live kept me silent.

> One of the first steps in learning to
> live with your kids when you've
> already lost your mind is to
> admit that you've already
> lost your mind.

I made a silent vow, standing there with my father's finger in my face, to never do that to my own children—but shortly after my fortieth birthday, I lost control of that finger. There I stood, wagging it in Traci's face, and at the same time asking her a question I didn't want her to answer: "Do you think I'm stupid?" Just by asking, I may have provided my own answer.

Children, in the first several years of their life, form attitudes and patterns that stay with them forever. During that same period, the minds of parents are also being reformed (or perhaps deformed) into new shapes. Parenting causes mental dysfunction. This is one of the first confessions we must make if we are to grow. Any parent who tries to offer a rational argument that his sanity has not been affected by raising children has probably raised *too many* children and totally lost touch with reality. Real parents, in fact, have great difficulty with rational arguments of any kind.

One of the first steps, then, in learning to live with your children when you've already lost your mind, is to admit that you've already lost your mind.

Confession Is Good for More than One Soul

Parents who can relax and admit their imperfections are much better able to make the adjustments necessary to be a good parent. Maybe that's why it's so healthy—and necessary—for us to maintain a sense of humor about ourselves, and even to laugh at ourselves now and then.

Parenthood is booby-trapped with emotional and intellectual mine fields that are best negotiated by moms and dads who don't stomp around in defensive ignorance. Pretending you're perfect detonates explosions that can alienate children, sabotage communication, and inflict casualties of conflict and guilt.

After writing *How to Live With Your Parents Without Losing Your Mind*, I began receiving invitations to conduct seminars on parent-teen relationships across the country. The answers to one of the questions in a survey given at those seminars revealed how badly our kids need to see vulnerability and humility in us. Over six hundred kids were asked what words they most wanted to hear from their parents. Of course, "I love you" was the overwhelming first choice. It was their *second* choice that caught me by surprise. These kids were desperate to hear their parents say, "I'm sorry. I was wrong." Not only is it okay for your children to see that you make mistakes, it is *essential to their well-being that they hear you admit it.* Such openness frees them to be open and honest. It frees them to take the kinds of risks inherent in effective living; it gives them the security of unconditional love, daily demonstrated through confession and forgiveness.

Perfectionism Encourages the Puppy Syndrome

An angry man approached me after one of my seminars. "I would *never* apologize to my children or admit that I'd been wrong," he blustered. "It would erode my authority." His fear that admitting he was wrong would cause his children to lose respect for him was a mark of his own insecurity. To the contrary, his rigid insistence on maintaining the illusion of perfection was not teaching respect; rather, he was teaching a paralyzing fear of failure, and also encouraging deception.

His approach reminds me of the man who was having a hard time housebreaking his puppy. The man demanded perfection. Each time he came home to find a mess on the floor, he would rub the dog's nose in his mistake and throw him down the front steps. But by a few weeks into the training, the man realized that his approach wasn't having the desired effect; the bewildered puppy continued to wet the floor, and every time the owner came home, the dog would rub his nose on the floor, run outside, and roll down the front steps. The puppy was obviously eager to please—but, somehow, he had lost track of the basic principle.

Our dog, Heidi, chose a more deceitful route. Every time we were gone for more than a few minutes, Heidi would leave a disgusting surprise somewhere in the house. We learned how to discover where she had committed her little crime—all we had to do was watch which room she avoided. She would romp and play as though nothing were wrong but would not even look in the direction of the room where her evil "duty" lay. If we entered the scene of the crime, she would wait timidly down the hall, peeking around the corner.

Behavior like that isn't limited to dogs, but I call it the "puppy syndrome"—a refusal to admit that any mistake has been made and a desperate need to cover up the mistake at all costs. We parents can infect our children with the puppy syndrome when we refuse to admit our own mistakes. Children who don't see modeled, in their own home, the freedom that comes with confession and forgiveness may learn to lie, to create elaborate schemes to cover up mistakes, or to desperately try to create the illusion of perfection.

One day, not long after I had asked Traci not to ride in the car with her newly licensed friend, I came home to a puppy-like greeting. Hugging me over and over (behavior uncharacteristic of Traci), she bubbled, "Daddy, we went downtown to rent a video, and I rode my bike." (Bike riding was also a behavior uncharacteristic of Traci.) Usually, the girls needed my help to get their bikes down from their storage place in the garage. Her eagerness to demonstrate to me, on the spot, how she could remove the bike and replace it all by herself caused my little "parent antenna" (equipment implanted in all parents who have seen their child lie) to hum with suspicion.

I turned to Taryn, Traci's younger sister. "Do you know how Traci got the video?" I asked.

"I'm not supposed to tell," she mumbled, avoiding eye contact with the car in question.

I quickly discovered the truth: Traci had, indeed, ridden with the new driver to get the video. The fact that she felt guilty for her disobedience was okay. Her desperate attempts at deception were not okay. But I was as much to blame for her deception as she was; by never confessing my own sins and mistakes, I had created an atmosphere that didn't allow for confession and forgiveness.

Our children know we aren't perfect. Every day, they see evidence of parental brain damage and of the inconsistencies in our lives. Our refusal to say "I'm sorry" for those things teaches our children that it is not acceptable to confess sins or admit mistakes. The more dangerous and subtle message is: Unless I am perfect, I will not be loved.

Life cannot be lived without making some mistakes; a life of faith cannot be lived without confessing them and seeking forgiveness. Your model of vulnerability frees your kids to take the chances required to live such a life. It helps them move toward independence and adulthood.

Vulnerability Encourages Honesty and Openness

One day I walked outside and found an old waterbed mattress filled to the bursting point, lying on our front lawn. Further investigation revealed that the hose was still running, quickly turning one of our window wells into a swimming pool. All of the evidence seemed to indicate that Traci had been playing with the garden hose, but when I questioned her, she vigorously denied it.

Her denial, I'm afraid, didn't convince me. Just a few days before, I had watched her climb to the top shelf of our closet and break a bottle of buttons. When I confronted her, she insisted that our dog had done it. Even when I told her that I had *watched* her do it, she still denied breaking the jar.

Because she had lied about the buttons, I didn't believe her about the garden hose. I sent her to her room for a year. (The initial sentence is always exaggerated because it gives me a lot of room to negotiate.) After she had served about two hours of her sentence, I discovered two little girls from across the street filling the window well with water. She had been telling the truth, after all.

My first thought was, *How am I going to save face?* But I quickly realized that saving face was not the issue. I had wrongly accused her and I needed to apologize. When I entered her room, Traci was sitting on the bed, still sobbing. She turned her head away from me, obviously deeply hurt, angry, and feeling helpless.

My status as a professional speaker couldn't help me now. I stood speechless, just inside the door of her room. "Traci," I called, but she refused to look at me. I sat on the bed next to her and confessed, "Traci, please forgive me for not believing you. I'm sorry, honey. I was wrong." I barely got those last words out of my mouth before she was in my arms.

I had *not* jeopardized my authority, as the man at my seminar had feared. If anything, I had strengthened it. The discussion that followed served as a turning point in our relationship. I explained how her previous lying had set us both up for this confrontation. I told her that I hated lies so much because they destroyed trust. I had her complete attention. It was the words "I'm sorry" that had brought her to my arms, and I'm convinced that those same words had opened her heart to the conversation that followed.

As she skipped out the door to play after our conversation had ended, she paused. "I'm sorry, Daddy—I lied about the buttons," she said. "I won't do it again."

I believe that my willingness to say "I'm sorry" freed her to do the same.

Personal Confession Demonstrates
God's Unconditional Love

A famous line from the movie *Love Story* goes, "Love means never having to say you're sorry." It made a great promotional gimmick for a movie, but as a representation of truth, it's lousy.

Saying you're sorry teaches honesty, open communication, and forgiveness. It's interesting that the man at my seminar who refused to apologize to his children was a minister. A child who has never seen confession and contrition modeled in his home may have difficulty accepting the grace of God. After all, the beginning of real faith is confession of our sins. We dare confess only when we know that forgiveness is available. As a parent, then, your model of confession and forgiveness is key in your child's ability to comprehend his relationship with God. Your willingness to admit your own weaknesses indicates to your kids that forgiveness must be available—otherwise, how could you dare be so open? That awareness frees them to believe that, if they are open, forgiveness might be available to them as well.

The first step in any twelve-step recovery program is to admit that there is a problem—more specifically, that *you* have a problem. You're not perfect—but that's okay. Why not admit your weaknesses, and confess your sins to God? Then, because you are secure in his forgiveness, you can have the courage to ask your kids for their forgiveness.

It isn't hard to admit that you're a parent—that fact is difficult to hide. But can you bring yourself to admit that you are an *imperfect* parent? Can you laugh at the evidence of brain damage so clear in all parents? Can you accept the challenge to make changes in your own life in order to improve your family?

If you can, then read on.

You Hold the Key to Change

Confession liberates you in another way: It opens the possibility of change in your own life—change that can revolutionize all of your relationships, including the relationships you have with your family.

"That's okay for dysfunctional homes," you may be saying, "but my home is okay just the way it is. We don't need that kind of change." In the only perfect home I know of, you can look out the window and see streets paved with gold and lions lying down with lambs. If you don't live there yet, then there's room for improvement.

A New Look at Authority

Most teenagers feel powerless to make significant changes in their home because they have no authority. A parent can come home from a conference or read a book and announce the changes she wants instituted in the home. A child has no such power. But parental authority is not a weapon to be wielded—it is a trust to be administered.

"How then," you may ask, "can I use my God-given authority to best affect my child?" You may not like the answer: Use your authority to change yourself. Nothing will be more effective in molding the character of your children than for them to see spiritual and emotional growth in *your* life. Improvements in parenting techniques will benefit and encourage your children—for a little while. But when things really get rough, it's the changes in your heart that make the difference—not the changes in parenting technique. Improving parenting techniques without making corresponding foundational changes of the heart is like building castles on sand. They'll stand until the first high tide, and then they're gone.

When a parent is willing to submit to the authority of Scripture and make the appropriate changes in his life, that parent provides a solid foundation for the spiritual and emotional growth of his children. We see our kids—and, thus, our role as parents—in a different light. Rather than using our authority to prove that we're still the boss, we can use it to make changes in our life that will strengthen our children.

In the national best-seller *The Seven Habits of Highly Effective People,* Stephen R. Covey exposes the shallow emptiness of quick-fix personal philosophies that promote outward changes without addressing the changes that are necessary within. He also points out the futility of using one's authority to try to change others:

> We began to realize that if we wanted to change the situation [with their son], we first had to change ourselves. . . . So we determined to focus our efforts on us—not on our techniques, but on our deepest motives and our perception of him. Instead of trying to change him, we tried to stand apart—to separate us from him and to sense his identity, individuality, separateness and worth. Through deep thought and the exercise of faith and prayer, we began to see our son in terms of his own uniqueness.[1]

Parental authority is not a weapon to be wielded. It is a trust to be administered.

One of the commonest (and easiest) ways we parents misuse our authority is by insisting that our children behave the way we want them to behave, forgetting to strengthen and develop their inner character. Covey says,

> I borrowed strength from my position of authority and forced her [his daughter] to do what I wanted her to do. But borrowing strength builds weakness. It builds weakness in the borrower because it reinforces dependence on external factors to get things done. It builds weakness in the person forced to acquiesce, stunting the development of independent reasoning, growth, and internal discipline. And finally, it builds weakness in the relationship. Fear replaces cooperation, and both people involved become more argumentative and defensive.[2]

When parenting techniques grow naturally from our desire to respond to our kids in a more Christ-like manner, then our responses will be consistent, rather than always exploding from the emotion of the moment. And our kids will take notice.

Candie Blankman, one of the most dynamic communicators in the country, told me a story that illustrates this truth. She had been preparing all day for a message she was to deliver later that week. Taken from the book of Habakkuk, the focus of her message was: *No matter how hard life might become, the righteous should live by faith.* In the midst of difficult circumstances, we should rejoice and find strength in the Lord. After complaining to God because of trouble at every turn, Habakkuk finally concludes.

> *Though the fig tree does not bud*
>   *and there are no grapes on the vines,*
> *though the olive crop fails*
>   *and the fields produce no food,*
> *though there are no sheep in the pen*
>   *and no cattle in the stalls,*
> *yet I will rejoice in the Lord,*
>   *I will be joyful in God my Savior.*
> *The Sovereign Lord is my strength;*
>   *he makes my feet like the feet of a deer,*
>   *he enables me to go on the heights.*

(Hab. 3:17–19)

Candie's bright young son Jeffrey chose an inopportune moment during her study to demonstrate some uncharacteristic bad behavior. The stress of preparing for her talk, combined with the distraction of her son's misbehavior, was too much. She responded in the same inconsiderate tone he was using and sent him to bed.

But later in the evening, Candie realized what she had done. She'd been preparing a message on finding joy in the midst of trouble and stress. Yet even while she was preparing that message, she was not demonstrating the principles she was about to teach. Instead, the very stress of preparing that message had caused her to snap at her son. She couldn't excuse his behavior—but neither could she excuse hers.

She slipped up the stairs and woke Jeffrey from a sound sleep. As he snuggled in her arms, half awake, she demonstrated the most important aspect of good parenting. "I'm sorry for the way I responded to you today," she said. "But there's something more important that I want you to know: It isn't enough just to know a lot about the Bible; you must allow what you know to *change* your life. Forgive me for not practicing what I was preparing to preach. From now on, I will try to let the joy of the Lord show through even when I'm under stress."

I believe that, deep within the heart of that sleepy boy, a subconscious root of truth took hold: *My mom has the freedom and authority to let God change her life. Maybe God can help me make changes in my life, too.* May that root of truth grow—and serve him well.

Making Change Is the Hard Part

A store owner was attempting to train a poorly educated young man for a job as a checkout clerk. When he asked the trainee how his day was going, the young man responded, "Puttin' money in is easy, and takin' money out is easy. It's makin' change that's the hard part."

In real life, too, the easy part is the everyday give-and-take, responding on impulse to the actions and reactions of our kids. The hard part is making change—changing our responses to be loving and consistent so that at the end of the day we still have a positive balance. Often, our first response to family stress is to pray that God will change our kids. And that's okay. Kids need to change and grow, and I would never discount the power of prayer. Those prayers are important and should be continued for as long as our kids breathe. But those prayers for our children should be supplemented by a more important prayer: "God, please give *me* the strength to change where *I* need to change." Although we have the power to insist on outward changes in the behavior of our children, the most important change we can make is the inward change in ourselves.

Burn the mental list you have of all the faults you see in your children. Instead, make a list of all the attitudes and habits in your own life that need to be addressed. Don't misunderstand—I'm not saying that you shouldn't establish behavioral guidelines for your children and enforce those guidelines with discipline. In fact, I'll encourage those actions in chapter 5. The problem is that we parents find it very tempting to hope that some list of rules, or some application of parenting technique, will miraculously change our family. Deep down, we know it doesn't work that way—but we're still frustrated to discover that, despite our authority to change our kids' outward behavior, we're helpless to change their basic character. Only *they* can change their basic character, with God's help—and they'll be most motivated to make those changes by seeing the results of such changes in you.

Parts Is Parts

Making changes in the basic character of any member of the family is something that touches the entire family. It's a little like the program in Diane's computer for projecting the financial outcome of a project. She can enter hundreds of projected expenses and sources of income, and after the entire program is set, a change in any one of those input columns immediately changes the final outcome. If I get impatient and try changing the final figure just because I want the results to be different, the computer won't allow it. Only by changing the individual input variables can I change the outcome. Or, expressed another way, the whole cannot be accessed except through the parts.

**You are the only part of the family
equation you can totally control.**

The same is true of your family. You will find only frustration in trying to change the final result without changing one of the parts. And guess which part is the *only* one you have the power to change?

The resulting changes in the family as a whole can be dramatic, but there are no guarantees in parenting. You may look deep into your soul, learn to love your family in a more meaningful way, and still not see any appreciable change in the behavior of any other member of the family. But because you have changed, the family as a unit will have changed. You are the only part of the equation that you can control. Allow God to change the attitudes and beliefs that control the way you respond to your kids, and you will have tapped the most powerful resource available to parents.

Hesitant to consider such changes because of the potential for personal pain? Reluctant to commit the time and effort required for making basic changes in yourself? (And make no mistake: Changing yourself *is* painful, and it *does* require time and effort.) Then consider the alternatives. You can leave things just the way they are—status quo. If that option were attractive to you, you probably wouldn't have bought this book. Or you can make things worse—not a choice many parents would intentionally make. Or you can change, building a foundation of love and respect from which successful parenting can spring. Only that last choice will give meaning to whatever parenting techniques you use and whatever behavioral guidelines you establish for your kids.

Will it be easy? No. Is it guaranteed to change some abhorrent behavior of another member of your family? No.

Will it bring you a deeper sense of peace as you seek to be a good parent? Yes. Will it decrease the tension in your home? Yes. Will it give you a better chance of molding the character of your children? Yes.

If you're asking, "Where do I start?" my answer is, "Turn the page."

2

Looking for Trouble

Finding Room for Improvement

I *am the key to change and growth in my family.* If you
agree with that statement, the next step is to act on it. If
we refuse to act, we don't simply preserve the status quo—we
amplify the problem. In gambling, it's called chasing losses: A
gambler losing money continues to gamble, hoping that some
miracle of luck will help him win back what he has lost. This is
the reason gambling is so destructive—most gamblers don't
quit until they have lost more than they can recover. Now is
the time to act.

But simply deciding to act isn't enough. Before you start a
journey, you need to know which direction to drive; before you
begin to grow into a more effective parent, you need to know
which areas need improvement.

Where Can I Start?

No one really enjoys finding out what he's doing wrong. Our
negative behavior often springs from deep-seated (sometimes
hidden) motives. When someone criticizes our words, actions,
decisions, or attitudes, we become defensive; we deny the
problem; we marshall all our forces to protect our fragile egos.
Our emotions quickly rise to the surface.

And those, of course, are good signs that our accuser is on the right track. If a family member points out an area of your life that you know needs change, your emotions may explode—and so may a number of blood vessels in your forehead. If there's anything harder than admitting you're wrong, it's having someone else—especially someone close to you—point out that you're wrong.

Even so, we need help from sources outside ourselves in spotting areas for improvement. We need to listen to our families, to others outside our families—and to God.

Listen to Your Family

I was lying in a hotel room seven hundred miles from home when the phone rang. It's good that I wasn't standing, because the news would have knocked me down. My wife Diane was calling to let me know that, because of a clerical oversight, we would have to pay a huge amount of unexpected tax.

Since Diane handles all the financial matters in our home and is in charge of clerical oversights, I exploded. "How could you let this happen!" I raved. "This is going to wipe out our entire savings!" Diane patiently listened while I ranted on for several minutes. "Thanks a lot!" I blurted finally, in a fit of immature frustration. "You've certainly ruined my day!" With a muttered curse, I hung up the phone.

I didn't sleep well that night. At first, I was worried and angry about the money we'd lost. But those feelings were quickly replaced by a deep concern for the way I had reacted. Under pressure, I always seem to get angry and take it out on the ones I love the most.

At the crack of dawn, I called home. Traci picked up the phone, and I explained that I wanted to apologize to her mom for losing my temper the night before. Her response went through my heart like a knife: "Mom told me you would go through the roof," she said. "But I knew that anyway. You always come unglued under pressure." With that, she handed the phone to her mother.

An angry response was on the tip of my tongue, but then I realized she was right. She hadn't said those words to hurt me. She had simply stated, matter-of-factly, what was true.

It's obvious—my family has me figured out. I'm so predict-able they can forecast my reactions. *When Dad finds out, watch out! Lightning will flash and thunder will roll!* They know that, too often, I allow circumstances to control my reactions. Therefore, when they observe the circumstance, they can predict the reaction.

I wish I could say to you that this income-tax explosion happened during my tender, immature years, early in my marriage. Unfortunately, it happened as I was writing this chapter. If you and I are to recognize the areas of our life that need improvement, we must be willing to listen to outside sources—sources like a daughter who can see the patterns in my behavior with more clarity than I can.

Listen to your children and spouse. Because they know you better than anyone else, they can help you identify specific areas of your life that need change.

You may discover, however, that your family members are hesitant to volunteer constructive criticism—especially if, in the past, you've reacted negatively or refused to listen to their suggestions. You may need to rebuild some bridges by asking, "Are there some areas in my life that, if changed, would make me a better parent?" If they answer, don't defend yourself or retaliate. Listen for the grain of truth, ask for elaboration or clarification, thank your spouse or child for the input—and then begin the difficult job of growth.

Do their judgments sound unfair? Remember that it is their *perceptions* that are important. If your children say that you constantly put them down, for instance, you may be tempted to defend yourself by pointing out all the times you build them up. But all of the self-defense in the world won't change the fact that your children *feel* put down. Instead of being defensive, ask, "What can I do to build you up more?"

When your family is convinced that you sincerely want to know how you can be a better parent and spouse, you'll hear valuable (and no doubt surprising) "inside intelligence"—most of which you'd probably never have heard if you hadn't been willing to listen. Just listen—it's a giant step in the right direction.

Listen to Others

Twenty years ago, a dear friend pointed out that, in a particular situation, I had been very inconsiderate to my wife.

Hurt by his comment, I snapped, "I don't think that's any of your business. And anyway, since you're not married, I don't think you have much counsel to offer."

Wrong again. Many years later, Diane and I found ourselves working through a difficult problem caused by the inconsiderate habits my friend had pointed out. If only I'd listened then.

Even when criticism seems undeserved, there's usually a grain of truth. Defend yourself against the criticism, and you gain nothing. Listen to it, and the most you risk, even if it turns out to be inaccurate, is a few moments of pain and a little time lost. It takes a strong parent to submit his personality to the grueling and painful search for personal excellence, but that kind of determination can change your family forever. Don't run from the insights of other people. Value them as perspectives from which you can see new, challenging dimensions for change.

Reading parenting books and attending parenting seminars and classes are other ways (perhaps less threatening ways) of gaining the perspective of other people. Unfortunately, in most families, those seminars and classes are usually attended only after trouble has already developed. Even when things are going well, grab all the continuing education on parenting you can get. There's a wealth of practical information available that will help you identify as many areas for improvement as you can handle. But remember: All the information in the world is of no value unless you're committed to act on it.

Listen to God

There is no more important source of information about ourselves; we must listen to God. We start by searching the Scriptures; then we allow what we read there to inform us about our life; then we allow God to empower us to take action.

The power to change years of habitual behavior must come from a source greater than myself; this I know from my own experience. Those changes are changes of the heart, and to make them, we need help from the expert in heart changes.

> *Unless the Lord builds the house,*
> *its builders labor in vain.*
> *Unless the Lord watches over the city,*
> *the watchmen stand guard in vain.*

> (Ps. 127:1)

That verse is as true for families as it is for houses and cities. On my own, for instance, I tend to be unforgiving and selfish. But the model of Christ's forgiveness in my own life has given me the strength to forgive others. I know myself; I know how little I deserve his love. By listening to his example and opening myself to his power, I am able to exercise forgiveness even when I don't want to.

Yes, it takes courage to lay your life before God and say, "Lord, show me where I need to be more like you. Show me where I am weak, and fill in those spots with your strength." If you pray that prayer, prepare to be showed, because God will respond. He will use other people, family members, your conscience, and the wisdom and power of his Word to answer your prayer. Psalm 139:23 is a prayer that I have said many times—and it has *always* been answered. Perhaps you will make it your daily prayer:

> *Search me, O God, and know my heart;*
> *test me and know my anxious thoughts.*
> *See if there is any offensive way in me,*
> *and lead me in the way everlasting.*

An Exercise in Listening

Parents who refuse to identify and act upon the areas of their life that need change are often suffering from their own loss of self-worth; they use their children as chips to win back self-esteem. If you don't like yourself and have never come to grips with your own unique place in God's plan, you may end up *depending* on your family to reinforce and demonstrate your worth.

After receiving an Academy Award, actor Kevin Costner was asked in a television interview, "Who are you?"

"I am defined by my family," he responded.

It was refreshing to see a Hollywood star acknowledge the importance of his family, but I truly hope he is not literally *defined* by that family. If he is, then when his children misbehave or do something stupid, Mr. Costner will see that as a blemish on his own image—as, indeed, many parents do. Those parents mean well, but they treat their children as I, to be honest, treated mine early in my experience as a father—as tools to build my own ego, as showpieces of my worth. It was only through the kind of listening that I've been discussing above that I became aware of that negative behavior and was able to do something about changing it.

That behavior began early in my career; I had been speaking for a living for just a year when I received an offer that I felt I couldn't refuse. A businessman asked whether I could come to Florida to speak at a convention. The cash register in my head lit up. At the time, my fees were about one hundred dollars a day, but I was sure that a large company like this could probably spring for *double* that amount.

But, bad luck—the dates he wanted came during our vacation. Diane insisted that I turn the offer down.

On three separate occasions, the man called to see whether I wouldn't change my mind. Frustrated, I thought of a way to get him off my back permanently: I made him an offer so ridiculous he would have to refuse. "I'll be glad to come," I told him, "if you'll pay me $1,500 dollars for the speech, pay airfare for Diane and Traci to come, and put us up, all expenses paid, in a nice place on the beach during the rest of the week so we won't miss any of our vacation."

I was silently chuckling and trying to imagine the look on his face when I heard him respond, "Great! We would be happy to. You'll come, then?"

What could I say? "Just kidding?" How was I going to explain this to Diane? I decided honesty was the best policy. I put my hand over the phone and called her into the room. "I'm in a fix," I stammered. "I tried to get this Florida guy off my back by offering to come if he would pay us $1,500 plus airfare and expenses to bring you and Traci down for our entire vacation at some nice place on the beach. He said *yes!* Now what do I do?"

"Take it, dummy," she said, and turned and left the room.

By the time we arrived in Florida, my nerves were raw. Because I was being paid so much, I felt that I had to produce a better show than ever before. The evening of my speech, I faced one of the most unruly groups I have ever seen. To make matters worse, the man who had originally invited me didn't show up, and my introduction was handled by a very inebriated stranger. "I don't know who our speaker is tonight," he said, "but I want you to sit down, shut up, and listen to him." Then he turned and continued a loud conversation with the women standing next to him.

Terrified, I stood to speak. But before I'd finished the first sentence, an uncontrollable nightmare began to unfold. Traci, who had been sitting in the back, broke loose from Diane and came lurching up the aisle with that Frankenstein walk only children (and monsters) are capable of. "Daddy, Daddy!" she slobbered as she staggered forward, a huge toothless grin on her face. To be honest, she looked a lot like some of the men sitting in that room.

I tried in vain to give her one of those parent looks that means, *Attention! You are in mortal danger unless you return to your mother.* Traci ignored me and continued her journey. Red with embarrassment, I said, "Traci, go back to your mother."

Immediately, someone in the audience shouted, "Let the kid up there! We want to see the kid!" Angry on the inside but trying to maintain my outward composure, I picked Traci up and between clenched teeth hissed, "Say hello; then return to your mother or I will personally donate your body to science." Undaunted, she grabbed the mike and said, "I want to sing!"

Few things in life are more difficult than trying to discipline a child in front of an audience. I had just begun to whisper hoarse threats when I heard another voice from the audience: "Let the kid sing! We want to hear the kid sing!"

Leaning out from my arms, both hands strangling the microphone, Traci began to sing the only song she knew:

"Jesus loves me, this I know," she sang, her eyes dancing with delight. "For the Bible tells me so!" By the time she reached the second verse she was in full form. Throwing her head back for the chorus, "Yeeeeeeesss! Jesus loves me! Yeeeeeeesss! Jesus loves meeeeee! The Bible tells me so."

To thunderous applause, Traci made her way back to her mother. And as I began my speech, there was more than one wet cheek in that audience. The whole atmosphere of the room had been transformed by a child's honest, musical declaration of simple faith. Those men listened with interest and respect as I delivered my address. And afterward, I spent more time talking to the men about the message of Traci's song than about the motivational content of my speech.

Yes, everything worked out fine that evening—but as I look back, I see the selfish actions and thoughts of a parent who was concerned about how his child affected his image. Insecure and hungering for success, I used my daughter to bolster my ego rather than loving her for who she was.

Think about it. At first, I was angry at Traci—I feared that her innocent, childish dash for the podium would be seen as a reflection on my character. *What will these people think? She's ruining my act!* I certainly had no other reason to be angry with her. She didn't disobey. She didn't run to me with the intention of disrupting my meeting or causing me embarrassment. She ran to me because she loved me and spontaneously wanted to express that love.

And as soon as the audience responded positively, I was no longer angry! How tragic! My response to my beloved daughter wasn't based on my love for her, or even on her behavior, but rather on the *audience's response* to her behavior. When she would run to me at home yelling, "Daddy, Daddy!" there was never a hint of anger. I would scoop her into my arms, rejoicing in her love. But onstage, my concern with my own ego overshadowed that spontaneous expression of love.

Over the years, I have counseled hundreds of teenagers and young adults who have expressed feelings of rejection because of similar incidents in their childhood. I can still see the tears of one young girl who, fearfully, confessed to her parents that she had been promiscuous and was, in fact, pregnant. She was desperate, at that moment, for forgiveness and help. She needed to be reassured that her parents still loved her. But her parents responded, "How could you do this to us? What will our friends think?"

Yes, that girl's family as a whole would undoubtedly experience some unpleasant consequences as a result of her actions. But the more important issue was that she had gravely hurt herself, and now she desperately needed forgiveness and love. It's unlikely that she had planned this action as an act of rebellion against her parents. It's far more likely that she had simply made some irresponsible decisions that would have far-reaching consequences. Her parents' response implied that, at least for the moment, their main concern was not the feelings of the heartbroken child standing before them, but the embarrassment that this incident would cause them.

These parents loved their child deeply; they were eventually able to forgive their daughter and help her through this crisis. But first they had to recognize that she was the child of a forgiving God, not simply a possession of their own, or an embarrassing blemish on their reputation. They also had to realize that forgiving their daughter was not the same as condoning her mistakes.

When we lived in Minnesota, a ten-year-old girl near our home was constantly going to parties accompanied by older dates—dressed, by her mother, in nylon stockings and makeup that added years to her appearance. I wondered what that mother had in mind for her daughter. I doubt that it was unwed pregnancy, but that's what happened.

As I talked to that mom, it became clear that she regarded her daughter as nothing more than an extension of her own ego, a possession. Through her daughter, she had been living out a social life that had been denied her when she was young. As a result, her daughter had never had the chance to play hide-and-seek, or stomp in mud puddles, or catch frogs. Instead, she'd been pushed directly into adulthood. It was tragic to see this sweet girl who should have been skipping rope dealing instead with the emotional trauma of having a baby and giving it up for adoption. Her greatest worry should have been a scraped knee. Instead, she was dealing with a bruised heart.

My own possessive and selfish attitude toward my daughter wasn't as visible as that at the corporate speaking incident in Florida, partly because it was hidden by the positive response of the audience. Had they reacted with embarrassed silence or disapproval rather than applause, I'm sure I would have responded more harshly.

Unfortunately, my possessiveness became much clearer several months later. By that time, because the reaction to her impromptu performance in Florida had been so positive, I had made her a regular part of my presentation. Every time I spoke at a camp or church group, I would call her up to sing "Jesus Loves Me." As I had hoped, the response was overwhelming. Audiences loved her.

One night as I spoke to a group of teenagers at a camp in northern Minnesota, I called her up to the stage to sing. But this night was different. From the stage, I could see her standing in the back, her eyes wide with fear, vigorously shaking her head *no*. Smiling to hide my annoyance, I called her again, with just enough threat in my voice that she would know I meant business.

"Traci! [ominous pause] Come up here now! [even more ominous pause] Don't make the people wait, honey! Come on!"

Whose feelings was I putting first? Obviously, my own feelings and the enjoyment of my audience came before the comfort and peace of mind of my daughter. I am ashamed to admit that I never even considered that she might be sick or uncomfortable. As I stood nervously waiting, my most conscious thought was that, in front of all these people, she was making me feel foolish. I was afraid that, to the audience, it might look as if I couldn't control my own kids. Finally, by intimidation, I got her to come to the front where she frantically whispered, "Daddy, please don't make me sing!"

To which I frantically whispered back, "I want you to do as you are told!" Then, with an apology to the audience I announced that Traci was going to sing.

"No," she said, close to tears.

Not willing to continue this confrontation in front of an audience, I whispered, "You go straight back to our trailer and straight to bed. We'll discuss this further when I've finished my meeting."

After she left, I finished my talk and spent several minutes in sensitive interaction with some of the young people who were hurting. I showed these strangers more caring sensitivity than I had displayed for my own daughter.

By the time I returned to the trailer, I'd forgotten about the incident. I prepared for bed in the darkness and was just climbing into bed when I heard her sobs. I opened the door to the little space where she slept, and she flung her arms around me and buried her head in my neck. "I really do love you, Daddy," she choked, "but please don't make me sing."

In that moment, she showed more maturity and sensitivity than I had shown all evening. She was weeping because she was afraid that I had misinterpreted her reluctance to sing as a lack of love for me. I, on the other hand, had never paused to consider her feelings. I had just wanted to make a good impression on my audience. I had used my child as a prop for my show, a possession rather than a person, a demonstration of my success.

Before you decide that I should be taken outside the city gates and stoned, please consider two things. First, I have always loved my daughters with heartrending intensity. Those who make poor parenting decisions aren't necessarily those who love their children the least. Sometimes it's the other way around. And second, with God's help, I'm changing.

Several years after the Minnesota camp incident, Traci accompanied me on a speaking trip to California. I told the audience a story I had told many times before: As a tiny girl, Traci had run from the house wearing only her skin. "Catch me, catch me!" she had yelled as she streaked down the block. Only when I caught her did I realize that I was wearing just my underwear. The kids in the audience rolled with laughter, as they always did when I told this story. And I remember seeing Traci laugh, as she always did when she heard it.

But that night I woke to the sound of her crying. "What's wrong?" I asked.

"Nothing," she responded. (She learned that technique from her mother.) Finally, after a great deal of coaxing and cuddling, it came out. "Please don't tell that story anymore," she said. "Everybody looks at me when you tell that story."

"That's because they think it's cute," I said, a typical grown-up way of looking at things. "They don't think badly of you."

"They think I'm stupid for doing it!" she cried.

And then I realized that, once again, I wasn't really listening to her. Because that story always got such a positive audience response, I was willing to jeopardize her feelings to keep it. I even tried to convince her that, if I didn't use names, they might think it was her *sister* who had done it. She wasn't convinced; she was sure they would intuitively know that it was her.

So that night I promised her that I would never tell that story again. She was barely able to say, "Thank you, Daddy," before she fell into a peaceful sleep.

Less than a month later, I was standing in the wings of a stage in Ocean City, New Jersey. Just as the emcee was beginning my introduction, Traci ran up and introduced me to a new friend. I offered to take them out for ice cream right after the show, and then I headed for the stage.

"Daddy!" she called.

I was almost to the stage, and the audience was already applauding, but I turned in time to hear her yell over the din: "Be sure to tell that story about me running naked down the street—and be sure to tell them it was me that did it!"

People often ask me: Aren't your kids embarrassed when you tell those stories? The answer is no, not any more. I have chosen to be sensitive to their feelings rather than indiscriminately using their lives as a source of material for my presentations. As a result, they have grown more relaxed about the stories I tell. The stories that they feel are too personal or embarrassing, you have never heard—and never will.

See—I think I'm learning!

Many parents struggle with the same problem that led me to cause such embarrassment and emotional stress for Traci. Without realizing it, we view our children as possessions, or as manifestations of our own worth. I say "we" because I still fight this temptation. Perhaps parents like me need to speak more often with other adults who have tried to conceive children but have not been able to; those barren adults would quickly tell us that a child is not a possession, but rather a miraculous gift from God: "Behold, children are a gift of the LORD; the fruit of the womb is a reward. Like arrows in the hand of a warrior, so are the children of one's youth" (Ps. 127:3–4 NASB).

It's true that your children, genealogically, are yours, members of your specific family. But in reality, they are *God's* children. We don't own our kids; rather, we are privileged to have them on loan for a short period of time. It is our privilege and responsibility to nurture them in the Lord until they are capable of fully expressing their own personhood.

But you will never be free to love your children as unique creations of God until you see yourself in that same light. Ray and Anne Ortland put it well in their contribution to the book *Parents and Teenagers*:

> Parents are children too—children of God. Only if they are relating rightly to God as His children, only if they have a good "Parent-child" relationship with Him, will they be able to relate rightly as parents to their own children.[1]

In the same book, Charles R. Swindoll says:

> It's hard to put the needs of your kids above your own needs. It's hard to serve your family. It's hard to say no to something you long to do or yes to something you'd rather not do. But Jesus Christ made the supreme sacrifice. Our heavenly Father was willing to give everything—even His own being—for us, His children. When we focus on His example, it puts our day-to-day decisions in a different light. Concentrate on being unselfish and having a servant's heart. Continue the heritage your heavenly Father began and pass it on to your children.[2]

As you experience God's forgiveness, you will be free to forgive. As you recognize your worth in his love, you will not need to use your family to affirm your worth. You will be free to unselfishly love your kids for who they are.

Don't Be Afraid to Learn From Your Failures

T. J. Watson, founder of IBM, said that success is on the far side of failure.

That's good news, because during your quest for excellence as a parent, you *will* make mistakes; you *will* fail at times. Don't be discouraged. Those errors are the stepping stones to success.

At home, we have a computer program that can guess the name of any animal you think of. It asks a series of questions that narrow the possibilities of size, habitat, and other variables until, finally, it announces the name of the animal—even though the person playing the game has never verbalized it. Nowadays, few people are able to stump this program. How did a computer program get so smart? It learned from its mistakes. When we first got the program, it could guess only a few animals. But every time it guessed wrong, the computer would ask the user a question: *How was I wrong? In what way does a frog differ from an alligator?* The user would type an answer, and the program would retain that information so that the computer would never make the same mistake again. Like the robot in the movie *Short Circuit,* the computer sought input; it requested as much information as possible in order to be as correct as possible in the future. Throughout this chapter, I've been suggesting that all parents do the same.

What would happen if that computer had responded the way we do when we discover that we're wrong? It would get angry, print out, "Well then just forget it!" and shut itself off. Of course, if it reacted that way, it would never learn anything. Maybe computers *are* smarter than people.

Computers, however, never experience emotional pain— and the search for excellence is painful because it is always accompanied by the intentional exposure and eradication of those behaviors and attitudes and beliefs that hinder our effectiveness. Growth as a parent means being willing to search for input that will help rid you of negative patterns in your life so that you'll be better equipped to help your kids grow and mature. To try to skip those difficult and painful changes and instead concentrate on mastering parenting techniques is an exercise in futility. Unless we deal with the attitudes that affect our behavior, it won't matter how many great parenting techniques we learn—we'll quickly revert to the old habits we've practiced for years. Those habits die only when they're pulled up by the roots.

My father was a prisoner of war, living near starvation, for three-and-a-half years. His waking hours were completely taken up with finding and hoarding food. Rotten rice and even insects were hidden—saved to be eaten later when hunger could no longer be ignored.

When his prison camp was liberated, planes flew over and dropped barrels full of food. One of those barrels landed in front of my father and broke open—scattering hundreds of candy bars on the ground in front of the starving prisoners. Surprisingly, few of those prisoners ate them immediately. Instead, they gathered as many as they could and stuffed them into their tattered clothing for later. Every one of those men knew that the war was over and that relief was already arriving, yet they couldn't break the hoarding habit they had developed over years of imprisonment.

Similarly, the way we respond to our children (especially teens and preteens) has become habitual; it has taken years to develop. Don't expect those habits to change overnight. It takes time to believe that the war is really over.

The process of ending that family war doesn't begin with your kids; it begins with you. And with God's help, you can begin right now.

3

No News Is Bad News

Keeping Communication Lines Open

Silence Isn't Golden—It's Deadly

It was 1985. I was flying in cold gray clouds at seven thousand feet, and I knew I was in trouble. An inch of deadly ice protruded from the leading edge of the airplane's wings. Icing like that had killed many pilots in the past, but I thought I could deal with it—so I began to climb.

Suddenly I smelled smoke. Within seconds, the white, acrid smoke from burning wire filled the cockpit and stung my eyes. Now the situation was critical. There's nothing more dangerous for a pilot than an in-flight fire. When it's combined with airframe icing in instrument conditions, the odds against survival are great.

Wasting no time, I radioed for help and received an immediate response. The controllers on the ground knew that my situation was grave. Because of the fire, I'd had to shut off the electrical instruments I desperately needed to fly in the clouds. I was flying blind in an airplane that was quickly turning into a popsicle. I had only one hope for survival: my link of communication with the controllers. I had to keep them appraised of my situation, and they had to keep me informed as to where I might land. Most of the airports within easy distance were closed because of the weather. Minneapolis had the nearest airport with the radar to guide me down and the fire equipment to assist if I was unsuccessful. By the time I reached Minneapolis, there would be no fuel left for a second try.

Even though it was a life-and-death situation, I felt assured that the controllers and I could work together to find the best solution to this mess. But that assurance was quickly shaken. In order to give me proper radar coverage, the controller asked me to change to a different radio frequency. He told me that I would be talking to people who would guide me all the way down to the runway. He encouraged me to stay calm, wished me luck, and gave me the new frequency. I quickly tuned it in and asked for help. Dead silence.

For five minutes (it seemed like five years), I called for help. Without communication, I was facing certain death. I didn't have enough gas to get to clear weather and (because of the fire) I didn't have the instrumentation I needed to land in this weather. Only communication with the controller could save my life. I switched back to the old frequency. No response.

Now I was terrified. I tried other frequencies, hoping I might run into one that would get me through. In my panic, I forgot the frequency I had originally been assigned. As I frantically twisted the dial my earphones were suddenly filled with the sweetest sound in all the earth: someone calling the numbers of my plane. The controller carefully guided my plane through the fog to a tense but safe landing at Minneapolis International Airport. If communication had not been restored that day, chances are great I would have become a sad statistic of what happens when people don't talk.[1]

That story from my own experience is reprinted from my book *How to Live With Your Parents Without Losing Your Mind* because I know of no other illustration that so graphically shows the importance of open communication.

Recently a father boasted to me, "I've got pretty good kids. I don't bother them and they don't bother me." His intentions may have been good, but that man was flying in dangerous territory with his radio off. I had just spent two hours with his son, who was lonely, alienated, and desperate to know whether his father really loved him.

"No news is bad news," I replied to that father. His brow wrinkled in confusion, just as yours probably did when you first read the title of this chapter. The point is this: If there's no communication, then you're getting no news—and that's bad news. Even the frustrating communication of conflict is better than no communication at all.

One of the reasons Iraq was so impotent against the coalition forces in the Gulf War was because Iraqi communication lines had been broken early in the conflict. Without communication from central command, morale quickly broke down. Helpless Iraqi soldiers surrendered by the thousands.

Lines of communication are no less important in a family. If there is communication, there is hope. That's why two chapters of this book will be devoted to establishing and keeping open good lines of communication.

Communication Is More Than Talking

There are three broad levels of communication that we use most as we talk to our kids. Although all three are essential to survival, there is one level of communication that is the most important to your children's emotional development—and that one, sadly, is often the most neglected. An understanding of those three levels and how they work should enable us to communicate better with our kids.

Level One: Informational Nagging

Informational nagging consists of giving orders or instructions and asking probing questions about whether those orders and instructions were followed.

"Empty the garbage!"

"Clean your room!"

"Brush your teeth!"

Those are examples of level-one communication. Orders and instructions like these are usually followed by questions like:

"Did you empty the garbage?"

"Is your room clean?"

"What's that growing on your teeth?"

Level-one communication is designed to get things done; it's absolutely essential in meeting the ordinary needs of everyday life, but it does little to draw you and your children closer together. Kids perceive it as nagging. H. Steven Glenn and

Jane Nelsen, in their book *Raising Self-Reliant Children in a Self-Indulgent World,* call this kind of language *adultisms.*

> An *adultism* occurs any time an adult forgets what it is like to be a child and then expects, demands, and requires of the child, who has never been an adult, to think, act, understand, see, and do things as an adult. These unrealistic expectations from adults produce impotence, frustration, hostility, and aggression in young people. They undercut the value of expressions of love. They destroy children's belief in their own capabilities, their sense of their own significance, and their influence over events. Still many of us commit adultisms with our children many times a day.
>
> The language of adultisms is, "Why can't you ever? How come you never? Surely you realize! How many times do I have to tell you? Why are you so childish? When will you ever grow up? Did you? Can you? Will you? Won't you? Are you? Aren't you?"[2]

Glenn and Nelsen say that we spend more then half of our communicating time with our children on this level. I'd say they're being conservative; I think we spend *almost all* of our communicating time on this level. How unfortunate! Even adults quickly tire of a constant barrage of level-one communication, and we're more aware than kids that it's a necessary evil. Our mail, our telephone conversations, our business discussions—our whole lives are filled with it. But level-one communication by itself avoids intimacy; it does nothing to enhance relationships. When the phone company calls to tell you that you missed your last payment and must remit immediately, you don't suddenly feel closer to the phone company because they cared enough to call. Even the notice you receive in the mail acknowledging that your bill has been paid doesn't make you want to call and set up lunch with the person who sent it. Level-one communication concerns rules and their enforcement. It is designed to get us to *do* something. Unfortunately, it usually bypasses the heart. As I write this, a small light is blinking on my computer, indicating that the battery is low. That is important information. It's also effective—I'm about to get up and plug my computer into a wall outlet. But I'm not drawn any closer to my computer through that communication.

My parents loved me very much, but in all the years of my childhood I can't remember a single conversation except those in which my parents were giving me an instruction, checking up on whether the instruction had been carried out, or informing me of the consequences of not carrying out that instruction. I have few regrets about my childhood—but oh, how I wish we could have communicated on a deeper level. I am glad, now that I am an adult, that my parents and I are able to communicate at a deeper level. And I hold no grudge against my parents, because I know it is difficult not to fall into this trap. In fact, I fight constantly (and not always success-fully) to keep from limiting my own communication with my children to the same level.

As Traci moved into her teen years, she withdrew and grew more sullen. This was so uncharacteristic that I was worried. One day Diane reminded me that, for several weeks, almost all of my communication with Traci had been negative, limited to reminding her of chores and reprimanding her for chores she hadn't done. At Diane's suggestion, I went to the florist and picked out two arrangements of flowers, one for each daugh-ter. I left them in their rooms with a note apologizing for being such a nag and promising to be more positive in my communication. The results: The spring returned to Traci's step, the beautiful smile came back, laughter and talking filled the house again.

The door to communication had been closing. I had to move beyond level one to open it up again.

Level Two: Intellectual Dialogue

Level-two communication is the free exchange of ideas. When kids feel the freedom to express their thoughts, they feel loved and important. Discussions of faith, politics, world events, and personal philosophy should occur frequently, with plenty of room for questions and doubt. These discussions are a beautiful springboard for keeping abreast of the issues your child is facing. They can give you an unobstructed view of your child's heart.

Almost all level-one communication is one-way communication. The parent gives the orders, asks the questions, or announces the consequences, and the kid responds with grunts, shrugs, eyeball rolls, or bursts of anger. Level-two communication is two-way communication. It allows for the exchange of differing opinions. It stimulates thinking. When parent and child disagree, the child who is accustomed to level-two communication knows that his views are respected. He won't hide what he believes; he will also be more apt to listen to a parent who is proposing a different point of view, because he has seen that listening skill modeled by his parent. Unfortunately, few children have the privilege of this rich exchange. Parents often squelch ideas that are not consistent with their own, thereby discouraging honesty. We mistakenly believe that if we immediately show displeasure when our children express an opinion different from our own, our children will change to our way of thinking. In reality, all we've done is discourage our children from talking about what they really feel. They quickly learn to keep quiet or simply to say what they think we want to hear; their opinion hasn't changed. And they will eventually ask themselves, *How reliable are my parent's opinions, since he never seems willing to test them against opposing viewpoints?* It is especially difficult for a Christian parent to listen to the questions and opinions of a child when those ideas run contrary to the values and tenets of our faith.

We parents must remember: Listening and trying to understand the ideas of our children is not the same as endorsing them. Listening gives you an invaluable opportunity to know exactly what your child is thinking and an even more valuable opportunity to suggest other rational options.

Interruption and condemnation stop that communication. I know a young man who, in his late teens, called his father from summer camp. "Dad, I'm in love!" he announced, to which his father responded, "You don't have any idea what love is." A few years have gone by since then, and that young man recently told me that since that day he has never talked to his father about the women in his life, although there were many times he wanted to. That misguided father missed a tremendous opportunity to be a factor in his son's dating life. He slammed the door to communication.

The other day, my daughter announced that she wanted to go to Harvard and study to be an attorney. What an opportunity for an idea exchange! But instead of letting her dream, instead of listening in as she shared her ideas, I cut her off with, "Couldn't you choose a more humane occupation?" (Apologies to my attorney friends. It's clearly an economic issue: I couldn't accept the financial devastation a Harvard education would bring to our family. Harvard is probably a fine school, but I don't have a fine bank account.) Harvard was out of the question, I told her. And then, instead of encouraging her to share what had driven her to choose Harvard and to explain her interest in law, I slammed the door even tighter: "You need good grades to get into Harvard," I insisted, effectively moving the conversation back to the informational nagging mode.

Paramedics always try to keep critically injured people talking. Somehow, conversation keeps the patient from submitting to the subtle temptation to give up. Do the same with your kids. Keep them talking. It will give you more opportunity to address their strange and dangerous ideas than a curt rebuttal would. In fact, if you're in the habit of cutting your children off when they say something you don't agree with, you probably don't even know what strange and dangerous ideas they have. Allowing your children to express their ideas without rebuttal or judgment earns you the right to express alternative ideas and solutions. The open exchange of ideas allows two-way traffic on the street of communication. It also gives your child the chance to move with confidence to the next level.

Level Three: Heart-to-Heart Dialogue

The third—and most important—level is the communication of feelings. Heart to heart. This communication can flow naturally out of levels one and two.

Mature communication on this level deepens relationships. If, for instance, a friend sends you a note that says, "Don't forget the business meeting Friday, 7:30 p.m." That is level-one communication. You've been informed, but your friendship hasn't been enhanced. If your friend adds, "Call me—I'm interested in what you think about the subject we'll be discussing." That's an invitation to level-two communication, the exchange of ideas. You are stimulated to think, and the relationship is strengthened because you know that your friend values your ideas. If your friend adds, "I've missed you lately—I'm looking forward to seeing you," you have communicated on all three levels. But the warmth and support that will enhance the relationship came from levels two and three. Encouraging, supportive feelings have been communicated.

Children can hardly hear enough of words like, *I love you. I'm proud of you. You're special.* And we often need to encourage our children to participate in level-three communication with us by prompting them with comments like: *You seem sad. You seem to be angry. I can see that you're disappointed.* There is little chance that they'll respond honestly, however, unless they're confident that they can speak without fear of retribution. In *Raising Self-Reliant Children in a Self-Indulgent World,* H. Steven Glenn and Jane Nelsen say:

> A dialogue is a meaningful exchange of perceptions in a non-threatening climate of support and genuine interest. Without engaging in genuine dialogue with people of importance to them, our young people find it difficult to perceive themselves as meaningful and significant. And yet, dialogue is surfacing in research as the foundation of critical thinking, moral and ethical development, judgmental maturity, bonding, closeness, and trust. . . .
>
> Three perceptions are necessary before closeness and trust can be established in a relationship:
> 1. This person is listening to me.
> 2. I can risk my perceptions and feelings here without being discounted for them.
> 3. This person's behavior toward me indicates that what I think or have to offer is significant.[3]

Parents can learn to use, even in confrontation, a tone of voice that's supportive rather than distant and informational. "I'm disappointed in your behavior. Please help me understand

ON HIS WAY OUTSIDE TO BE PUNISHED FOR
MISBEHAVING, HERBIE LEARNS TO USE THE SYSTEM.

why you chose to disobey," is so much healthier than a level-one response: "How many times have I told you not to do that? What do you have to say for yourself, young man?" Our kids don't bother to give us meaningful answers to questions like that, because they know we're not really interested in listening. Level-three communication strives for mutual respect. It deepens relationships and invites resolution.

Open the Door Early

Communicating effectively with our children on all these levels requires effort—and, to be most effective, it should begin early in a child's life. Even before they can speak a word, kids begin to communicate with grunts, groans, and screams that require acknowledgement. (By the time they've become teenagers, of course, they'll have reverted to grunts, groans, and screams once again.)

At the height of her pea-smashing years, my daughter would spend great amounts of time talking to her pea before she destroyed it. There were no actual words that a human being could understand, but the babbling took on tones that were obviously meaningful. You could hear the sympathy in her voice as she rolled the pea gently between her fingers. "Dia gumba ben dowa neboten lack," she would murmur. (Translation: Prepare to die, little pea.) Then, with a glint in her eye, she would smash the pea to oblivion between her chubby fingers. "Dia gumba ben dowa neboten lack!" she would squeal. (Translation: Take that, you ugly little vegetable.) A look of surprise and astonishment would come to her face. "Uhhh," she would proclaim, stretching every fiber of her body toward me, smashed pea hanging precariously from the end of her finger. (Translation: Look at what I have done.) "Ughh?" she would ask, shifting her gaze from me to the pea. (Translation: Is it dead?) Finally, in a convulsion of giggles, she would stuff the remains of the pea in the remotest corner of her right ear. "Uhhh Bagga Boo!" she'd declare. (Translation: I must be the cutest child you have ever observed.)

Even at this early age, the way you respond to your children begins to establish the patterns of communication you will use in the future. I know—it's hard to communicate meaningfully with a three-foot human who speaks to vegetables. But your failure to at least acknowledge your child's efforts at communication may teach them that you have no interest in matters important to little kids (matters like vegetable capital punishment).

One of our first concerns with our children, of course, is table manners: "Don't play with your food!" (Informational nagging.) Table manners are an important concern, it's true—but parents would be wise to begin by acknowledging the death of the pea, thus building lines of communication that will be useful in helping to build table manners a little later. (Of course, it *is* important to work toward changing this pea-smashing behavior; otherwise, she might start smashing Cheerios, and then you'd have a cereal killer on your hands.)

Too often, the verbal bombs we parents drop intending to correct behavior (such as table manners) destroy instead the lines of communication by which such behavior can be corrected. If the child is exploring the depths of a toilet bowl, swinging a fork at a sibling, or digging in a light socket with a nail file, then of course a shrill, level-one "STOP!" is in order. For smaller children, a careful swat on the rear is often necessary just to get their attention before communication can begin. But, as a general rule, level-one communication without the accompanying level-two and level-three validation and affirmation will not accomplish the behavior-shaping that you're trying to achieve. It may, in fact, be counterproductive.

I'm not an advocate of either permissive or authoritarian parenting. Both take the easy way out. The permissive parent just ignores the actions of her kid; the authoritarian parent allows no response. A more difficult—but more effective—approach is trying to find the balance that allows the communication lines to stay open so that you will always have access to the heart of your child.

Keep the lines of communication open. The frustrations of dealing with kids who have begun to express their own feelings often causes parents to take one of the easy routes, becoming either permissive or authoritarian. Relax; accept the challenge to interact with this little relative. You were perfectly willing to do that when your child first arrived.

Do you remember that time? Do you remember the time before you'd lost your mind, when you were still relaxed with your children? Think of those times when you would read to them; the communication lines were wide open. You would only get as far as "Once upon a time there were three bears" when, with an excited squeal, your child would stab a finger at the picture in the book. "Bear," you would carefully enunciate, in that odd and tender tone of voice parents use only with their children. "That's a bear."

"Ughh," your child would respond.

Too often we drop verbal bombs
aimed at the behavior we wish
to correct but instead
destroy the communication lines by
which the behavior can be corrected.

Then, rather than rushing through the story, you would stop at the next picture of a bear and ask, "Where's the bear?"

After a moment's hesitation, and a look at your face for reassurance, the finger would fly out one more time. "Ughh?"

"Yes," you would exclaim. "I'm so proud of you!" And you were, even over something as simple as being able to tell a bear from a bowl of porridge. No commands, no nagging, just the free exchange of information—and encouragement by the bucketload. If your child pointed to Goldilocks when you asked, "Where's the bear?" you didn't slap his hand or scold him. You encouraged further pointing, so that you could show the difference between Goldilocks and the bear.

Many teenagers stopped communicating with their parents long ago. Why? Because every time they tried to express what they were feeling, someone slapped their hand.

Start early and never stop. Show interest in your kid's ideas, and learn to disagree without condemnation. Showing respect for a child's ideas isn't always easy. And it doesn't get easier as they get older—it just gets more rewarding. Far too many parents shut and lock the door to communication early in a child's life. When that child reaches adolescence, we wonder why we can't get it back open.

There is hope. There is always hope. Reestablishing broken communication with an adolescent—or even establishing strong communication habits with a toddler—is a difficult challenge. But even if you've already lost your mind, you can accept that challenge.

The lines of communication with your children are lifelines. Tend them well.

4

Learning to Talk Gooder

Basic Communication Skills

C ommunication is difficult. I've studied it, I teach its
principles all over the world, and I have practiced it with
spouse and child for over twenty years, and it's still one of the
most frustrating and complex challenges I've ever faced.

Communicating with your kids is like driving down a two-
way street with no lane markings—a precarious and uniquely
complicated trip at best, due to the differing perceptions of you
and your kids. Head-on collisions are a distinct possibility.
That's why many parents just give up and post one-way signs
all along the road:

"From now on I'll do all the talking, you just listen."

"Shut up and just do what I say.
I don't want to hear any of your questions."

The one-way signs our children see us putting up shut down
communication, rather than facilitating it. Perhaps we can
take down a few of those signs if we can just grasp the basic
skills of inter-family communications—skills that may help
keep you and your kids talking.

If You Want to Talk to the Natives, You've Gotta Learn the Language

As your kids grow, they develop a vocabulary that may sound like a foreign language. If you want to keep the lines of communication open, you'll have to adjust not only to the language, but also to the subtle nuances of tone and body language (both yours and your child's) that communicate so much.

My daughter Taryn flew into the room in a new outfit. "How do you like my dress?" she asked.

Those of you with wives and daughters know that this is a loaded question, almost impossible to answer correctly on the first try. "It's fine" I answered, meaning that it met my standards for decency, was functional, and looked good.

"You hate it!" she pouted. In her mind, "fine" is what you say to someone when you've taken the conversation—and the relationship—about as far as you want to take it. As in, "Fine! Have it your way!"

To communicate to her that I really *liked* the dress, I had to use language that *she* understood as complimentary. "That's a rad dress, Taryn, and it makes you look, like, totally beautiful."

"Thank you!" she said, and ran from the room beaming.

No, I'm not suggesting that you have to adopt the vocabulary of your kids. There's no need to ever force yourself to say the words *rad* or *gnarly* or to put your response in the form of a rap song, complete with all the right moves. I never use the word *rad* in casual conversation, but I'm perfectly willing to speak my daughter's language so that she'll know I like her dress.

Adults, after all, demand the same language clarification. If you want to tell your wife she has a face that makes time stand still, but you say, "Honey, you've got a face that would stop a clock," you're in trouble, no matter how good your intentions. If Diane asks me how she looks and I respond with, "Okay," she changes clothes. She's not confident that I mean it unless I use the descriptive language she understands as complimentary.

Informational nagging—the level-one communication we

discussed in chapter 3—short-circuits communication with adolescents by ignoring the feelings and language of kids. Questions like, "How many times have I told you?" require no answer. In fact, an answer to that question could trigger an angry and unhealthy parental response. No wonder kids resort to shrugs and grunts in response to our foreign adultisms.

> The habitual use of adultisms begins like this: "Why can't you clean up your room?" This adult has forgotten what it was like to be a child. Steve remembers his room when he was a child. It was the center of his mother's universe, but to him it was only a pit stop on his way to immortality. From that perspective, consider a typical exchange between Steve and his mother during Steve's adolescence:
>
> She would say, "Clean your room."
>
> Steve would say, "I did," meaning I have passed through it twice without tripping.
>
> She would say, "No, you didn't," meaning she could not eat off the floor. "What will the neighbors think?"
>
> The child's view and the adult's view were utterly irreconcilable.[1]

When our kids are little, we intuitively seek to understand the world from their perspective and to use the language they understand. When they are babies, we coo and cluck like idiots because they respond to that language. Remember how you emphasized Papa Bear's B-I-I-I-G bowl of soup when reading them a story? My mom knew how to get me to understand just by changing her tone. I would be running in the yard, playing a game that I never wanted to stop, when I would hear her voice: "K-e-e-ennn," she would call, the sweet, lilting tones drifting across the yard, music to my ears as I continued my game without responding. It was just nice to know Mom was there. After about three calls, the tone of her voice would take on a certain urgency. The screen door would blow completely open as she pronounced each syllable of my full name with exceptional clarity and power: "KEN-NETH AL-PHE-US DA-VIS!" As if by magic, I would appear on the doorstep before that last syllable died from her lips. She was speaking my language.

Let's not lose that intuitive urge as our kids get older. If we want to do more than simply get them to the supper table or express anger, it's well worth the effort to find the tone and the language that will help them understand what we really mean and that we really care. Finding the language that will help us find out what's inside their hearts will take even more time and effort.

Timing Is Everything

Unless we can recognize the moods of our children, it will be difficult to time our communication for maximum effect.

When Diane was pregnant with Taryn, our second child, I was deliriously happy. One day toward the end of her pregnancy, I told her that in my eyes she had never looked more beautiful. As I picked myself up off the floor, I was keenly aware that she had not taken my comment in the spirit given. She didn't feel at all pretty or attractive; the emotions of pregnancy, a rearranged figure, and twenty unwanted pounds had damaged her self-esteem. Not the best moment to step up with a cherubic smile and tell her that this is as good as she has ever looked. Regardless of what I meant, she heard something entirely different. My timing was wrong.

Teenagers, in particular, are subject to moods swings that can make living in the same county with them difficult. A poor grade or rejection by a friend can put them in a stormy mood that garbles any attempt to communicate. As in flying, it's always better to wait till the weather clears before trying to navigate the airways. Don't worry, you won't have to wait long. Sometimes the storm will pass in seconds.

Every year, as part of my career, I'm asked to provide entertainment on a cruise ship. (Hey—*somebody* has to do it.) Each time, I take one of my daughters with me. Those cruises give us time to be alone together without the usual interruptions. About midnight, at the end of a relaxed and happy day, Taryn and I entered our cabin to pack for the trip home. She stood leaning against the door with a dreamy smile; it had been a great week. "May I see your airline ticket?" I asked. "I want to make sure we have it ready for tomorrow."

She looked as if I'd hit her with a bucket of cold water. "I don't have the ticket!" she wailed. "You have it!" She slid to the floor, weeping uncontrollably. No amount of logic or coaxing could persuade her to simply look in her duffel bag to see whether it was there. With a great deal of wailing and gnashing of teeth, she argued that I had the ticket. Finally, when I insisted (I asked her how far she could swim), she attacked her duffel bag like an angry badger digging a new den. Within seconds, the ticket was in her hand; the tears and theatrics were instantly gone, and she said matter-of-factly, "Oh, here it is."

Now that she was sane, I asked what had so upset her.

"I didn't remember what happened to the ticket," she said. "I was afraid I might have lost it." It was midnight, she was dead tired, and the thought of a frantic search for a ticket that might not be there was more than her twelve-year-old body could handle. She didn't dare look in the bag; she might discover that her worst fears were true.

Now that everything was fine, she had just enough energy to pack her bags and crawl into bed. I lay awake, wondering about the workings of a child's mind and wishing we could shed worries and anxieties as easily as they can.

Watch for mood swings that inhibit or enhance communication, and time your words for maximum effect.

Learn to Listen

The greatest communication tool God created is not your lips. It's your ears. We are often so intent on giving our children advice and instruction that we forget to listen; we miss the clues that would tell us what advice and instruction they need the most. And when they've spoken to us, we respond before we've really considered the thoughts behind their words—or else we're so busy thinking up our response we don't even really hear what they're saying. Or worse, we don't give them a chance to say anything. Steven Covey tells the following story that illustrates this problem:

Two battleships assigned to the training squadron had been at sea on maneuvers in heavy weather for several days. I was serving on the lead battleship and was on watch on the bridge as night fell. The visibility was poor with patchy fog, so the captain remained on the bridge keeping an eye on all activities.

Shortly after dark, the lookout on the wing of the bridge reported, "Light, bearing on the starboard bow."

"Is it steady or moving astern?' the captain called out.

Lookout replied, "Steady, captain," which meant we were on a dangerous collision course with that ship.

The captain then called to the signalman, "Signal that ship: We are on a collision course, advise you change course 20 degrees."

Back came a signal, "Advisable for you to change course 20 degrees."

The captain said, "Send, I'm a captain, change course 20 degrees."

"I'm a seaman second class," came the reply. "You had better change course 20 degrees."

By that time, the captain was furious. He spat out. "Send, I'm a battleship. Change course 20 degrees."

Back came the flashing light, "I'm a lighthouse."

We changed course.[2]

**The greatest communication tool God
created is your ears.**

That illustration is far too characteristic of many of the conversations I've had with my kids. If only we would stop to listen. One evening as I walked in the door, I found Taryn, who was about five years old at the time, with a piece of fishing line tied to her tooth. The other end was tied to a door knob. I watched in amazement as she swung the door shut. The string yanked her head forward without dislodging the tooth.

"What are you doing?" I asked.

She shot me one of those *What insect are you?* looks and replied, "I'm pulling my tooth." She gave the door another swing. The twang of the fishing line snapped the hairs on the back of my neck to full attention.

"Let me see your tooth," I said, testing its condition with my finger. "It isn't even loose!"

"It will be," she said, giving the door another mighty swing. TWAAANNNG. Strained to the breaking point, several hairs fell from the back of my neck.

"Stop that!" I demanded.

"Leave me alone," she pleaded. "I need money!"

She needed money. Her real concern was so camouflaged by her actions that I would never have found it without a little listening. Not that she was trying to hide her real need—it's just that, having used kid logic to figure out how to creatively get what she wanted, she became intent on her task. She must have been using kid logic, too, when I asked her why she didn't just ask me for the money. She responded, "You weren't home."

It's hard enough to listen when kids know what they want to tell you; it's even harder when they don't know themselves. And often, kids are unaware of the source of their feelings. Especially with teenagers, it's important to seek to understand before seeking to be understood. And that means that parents must develop the skill of listening.

Shortly after his daughter Kari began dating, Daniel noticed that she was becoming moody and difficult. One night, she insisted that he was far too strict and hinted that she might run away. Actually, Daniel had been relaxing some of the rules to allow Kari the opportunity to exercise more responsibility. Now he was angry at what seemed to be an ungrateful attempt to push for no rules at all.

His first inclination was to storm into Kari's room and give her a piece of his mind. He'd show her the *real* meaning of strict. Instead, he decided to try to understand why she was so upset. He decided to listen.

Sitting on the floor next to Kari, he said that he had noticed her sadness and that he was aware of her tension over some of the rules. "What can I do to help you?" he asked.

Silence.

"Which rules are causing you the most frustration?" he tried again.

"I don't know," Kari answered.

Although Daniel was angry at her lack of effort to communicate, he fought the temptation to give up. Instead, he began to list the rules, one by one. Only two rules seemed to cause her trouble, and together they quickly agreed to some minor adjustments that might help relieve the tension. Thinking the issue resolved, he hugged his daughter and was about to leave the room when he stopped. Kari still looked so sad. Now, because he was willing to listen, he was hearing words of anguish that weren't even being spoken. But his willingness to listen encouraged her to speak. He walked back and put his arms around his daughter.

"I'm so scared, Dad," Kari cried.

"What's wrong, honey?" he asked. "What are you feeling?"

The tears rolled freely as she described the pressure she felt. But neither Daniel nor Kari could identify its source.

"How long have you been feeling this way?" he asked.

"About three weeks, I guess," she answered.

Pay dirt. Three weeks was the amount of time she had been dating. Kari wasn't quite ready, it appeared, for the new social pressures and responsibilities that accompanied her new dating relationship. Her resistance to Daniel's rules had simply become the outlet for her unidentified frustration. Just as with my little tooth puller, the problem was hidden by the way the child dealt with it. A little gentle digging and a lot of careful listening exposed the source of the trouble—not only to Daniel, but to Kari as well.

This kind of communication doesn't come easy; it requires a preexisting bedrock of trust and open communication. Questions from the parent must be asked without threat, accusation, or demand. Answers must be accepted without criticism or interruption. The goal is to discover the source of hurt and confusion in the heart of a child who may not even know the source of those feelings. What looks like confusion may really be guilt; frustration and stress may show up as misdirected anger. You'll never discover the real problem unless you seek first to understand.

Lynn told her group an amusing story about the time she asked her six-year-old son whether there were any black children in his class. He nodded and said, "Yes." She then asked if he played with them and he said, "No." Assuming he was acting out of prejudice, she gave him a long lecture on racial equality and tolerance and he squirmed the whole time. When she was finished, he gave her one of those "boy-are-mothers-dumb" looks and said, "Mom, we don't play with her 'cause she's a girl."[3]

Too often, we try to communicate with our children when all our lines are busy; we have our own agenda that keeps us from hearing what our kids are saying. The result is that we address problems that don't exist and miss hidden issues that are at the heart of the problem. Remember the story about the worker who asked a passerby to help him move a piano? With one of them on each end, they struggled for several minutes with the piano right in the middle of the stairway, but it wouldn't budge. Finally, the helper said, "We'd better get more help or we'll never get this piano up these steps."

Seek first to understand, then to be understood.

"*Up* the steps!" exclaimed the astonished worker. "I'm trying to get the piano *down* the steps!"

The helper had come with his own agenda; he didn't stop to find out what the worker needed. If Daniel had walked into Kari's room with his own agenda, I can guarantee he would never have discovered the real source of her pain. Seek first to understand, then to be understood.

Shhh . . . *listen!*

The Eyes Have It

It's possible for parents and children to say a lot of words to each other and not be communicating at all. It's also possible to utter not a word and communicate volumes. Whether you're speaking or not, eye contact with your child is crucial in communication.

That's especially true when you're engaged in confrontive communication; eye contact can reinforce your love even when your words are firm and businesslike. Several years ago, I attended an acting class in Hollywood. One exercise required that I look into the lens of a camera and say the words "I hate you"—while attempting to communicate the deepest love I could imagine. Talk about hard!

"I hate you," I would say, with a sing-song wimpiness that was supposed to register love. Instead, it made the declaration of hate sound all the more detestable. I tried shaking my head to indicate that I really didn't mean it, but that also seemed to emphasize the hatred.

Finally I gave up. The acting coach came to my assistance. "It's in the eyes," she said. "Say the words 'I hate you,' but show the love with your eyes."

When I saw the result on the screen, I was astounded. It was true: The eyes overruled those dreadful words. When the eyes said *love*, the "I hate you" became a mischievous expression of love. I would never, of course, recommend that you say those soul-scorching words to your own child even in play, but I would recommend that you establish eye contact with your child when you communicate. If love is there, the eyes will reveal it. If you find yourself wondering whether the love *is* still there, delay the communication until you're in control.

Eye contact also reveals much about what is happening inside your child. There's a reason you say to your child, "Look at me when I'm talking to you." It's because you want to be able to see, by the expression you see in their eyes, what's happening in their soul. How clearly lies show in the eyes of a child who can usually look at you with unclouded vision. Shame and defeat are all there for you to read—but you must look, or you'll never see what's written there.

A mother from Kalamazoo, Michigan, insisted that her daughter go to the doctor. Her daughter insisted that nothing was wrong, and in fact the girl was behaving normally in every respect but one: The life had disappeared from the girl's eyes. To the mother, the listless look in her daughter's eyes reminded her of the way her daughter had looked as a child when she was ravaged by high fever. The doctor found nothing

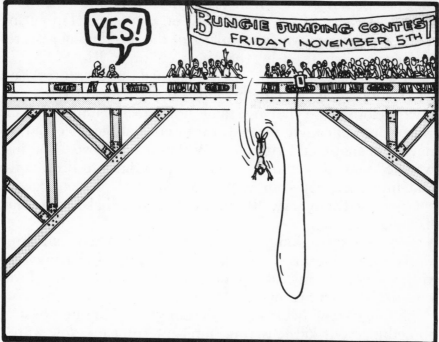

THE OLD CLICHÉS LOSE THEIR PUNCH.

physically wrong, but he took some time to do a little gentle probing. He found that this little girl was suffering from severe depression and that she was, in fact, considering suicide. The family attended counseling, and eventually the daughter emerged from her depression. Eye contact with a loving, sensitive parent may have saved her life.

Watch the Nonverbals

Kids are experts at reading your face. As I walk in the door, Taryn will shout, "What's wrong, Dad?" while talking on the phone and eating a Twinkie. Just one glance, and she knows its been a tough day.

It works in reverse, too, of course. Have you ever been angered by the nonverbal communication of your teenager? That slow release of air through pursed lips when asked to do a chore, the eyeballs that roll to the upper corners of their sockets, accompanied by the slight tilt of the head. More than one parent has been driven to distraction by the cluck of a tongue or shrug of the shoulders. You know what I'm talking about—right now, you're thinking of the maddening gestures and expressions used by your own children. Right?

Now where do you suppose they learned those gestures? You don't suppose it has anything to do with the fact that we unconsciously use the very same nonverbal communication? Have you ever caught the eye of your child at the table, only to have him freeze and grumble, "What's wrong now?" You just watched your son cram a whole bran muffin into his mouth, and unconsciously your displeasure showed on your face.

One day Taryn said, "I hate it when you shake your head like that."

"I do no such thing," I protested, only to have all three women leap to testify against me. Apparently, I shake my head very slowly when my kids do something to disappoint me. I was completely unaware of it.

Although your heart may turn completely upside down at something your kid tells you, don't interrupt the flow with a look of disgust or gasp of horror. If you immediately react with anger or shock every time there's a revelation, soon the revelations will stop. You can communicate your concern or advice much more powerfully and effectively if you're careful not to throw up barriers to communication first with nonverbal expression that threatens or angers your child.

Allow the Expression of Anger

I grew up in a home where the expression of anger was considered an act of rebellion—a common attitude in many families at that time. Unfortunately, that's still true in many families. Since teens and preteens spend a good part of their life feeling angry, you must allow for the expression of anger if you want your kid to talk to you at all.

The best treatment of the subject of teenage anger I have seen is in Ross Campbell's excellent book, *How to Really Love Your Teenager.* Dr. Campbell explains that one of the worst behavioral problems he encounters in teenagers—passive-aggressive behavior—is the result of unexpressed anger.

> Passive-aggressive behavior is the opposite of an open, honest, direct, and verbal expression of anger. Passive-aggressive behavior is an expression of anger that gets back at a person indirectly. A few examples of this are procrastination, dawdling, stubbornness, intentional inefficiency, and "forgetfulness." The subconscious purpose of passive-aggressive behavior is to upset the parents or parent figures and to make them angry. Passive-aggressive techniques of handling anger are indirect, cunning, self-defeating, and destructive. Unfortunately, passive-aggressive behavior is subconsciously motivated; that is, the child is not consciously aware that he is using this resistant, obstructive behavior to release his pent-up anger to upset his parents.[4]

Dr. Campbell explains that, the more the parents punish the child for such behavior, the more he will misbehave, because the subconscious motive of passive-aggressive behavior is to upset the parents. Anger must have some kind of expression. If you don't allow your kids to find an acceptable way to express their anger, it will fester and grow and find its expression in another (usually negative) way.

Being willing to listen to the verbal expressions of anger from your children and actively working to move them to more appropriate expressions of anger is difficult. A typical father at a parenting seminar said, "It's okay for my kid to be angry—I just don't want him to express it." Nothing causes my blood to boil more than the disrespectful tone of an angry child. But I would be wise to suffer the immediate discomfort of those angry words if by doing so I can avoid the long-term destruction that can result if there is no outlet for a child's anger.

Not long ago I sat with a boy who has spent the last several years in prison for shooting two people in the back. As this young man told me his story, he said several times that he'd never been allowed to express the rage that burned in his soul. For the first fifteen years of his life, he'd never raised his voice or spoken an angry word to anyone. But anger, unexpressed, unrelieved, was growing like a cancer in his heart. Rather than express those feelings, he would fantasize about the vengeance he would reap on the people who made him angry.

After years of keeping his anger bottled up, he remembers the exact moment that the fantasy switched to reality. By that time, the anger had crystallized into such concentrated hatred that it found its expression in the cold-blooded murder of two friends.

The most amazing part of this boy's story is the transformation that took place in his life because of the forgiveness of Christ. When he discovered that he could express his disappointment and anger to God and still be forgiven and loved by him, it was as though a crushing stone had been lifted from his body. An evil spirit had been exorcised from his life.

Not all children who find no other outlet for their anger will explode and kill somebody. But many will be driven to manipulative, passive-aggressive behavior: poor grades, doing a poor job on housework, skipping chores, dressing sloppily, and so on. This behavior brings discord; it can destroy families. Dr. Campbell explains why it is so common:

> Most people do not understand anger or know what to do with it. They feel that anger is somehow wrong or sinful and should be "disciplined" out of the child. This is a serious misunderstanding, because the feeling of anger is normal and has been

encountered by every person who has ever been born. If when your child becomes angry you spank him, or yell at him: "Stop that kind of talk. I will not allow it!" what can the child do? Only two things—he can disobey you and continue to "talk that way," or obey you and "stop talking that way." If he chooses the latter and ceases to express his anger, the anger will not go away. The child will simply suppress the anger into his subconscious, where it will remain unresolved and waiting to be expressed later through inappropriate and/or passive-aggressive behavior.[5]

Anger is not a sin, nor is the appropriate expression of anger a sin. Jesus expressed anger on several occasions. In James 1:19, the Bible instructs us to be *slow* to anger; in Ephesians 4:26, we are told to be angry *without sin*.

Allow your kids to tell you that they're mad. That doesn't mean that you have to let them become maniacal tyrants that rage about the house, destroying property and terrorizing siblings and pets. In fact, it's important not to allow destructive patterns of behavior to continue. Firm and consistent discipline for inappropriate expression of anger is vital as a foundation for teaching appropriate expression of anger. Campbell emphasizes that it is the *verbal* expression of anger that should be encouraged. Other than the vein-bursting desire it raises in a parent to wring some necks, there is little damage done even by inappropriate verbal expressions of anger.

By looking for the tiniest positive choice our kids are making in their expression of anger and encouraging and building on it, it's possible to progressively help our children learn to express anger appropriately. The "anger ladder" presented on the following page, developed by Dr. Campbell, illustrates the progression of steps in learning to express anger appropriately.

Remember: The goal is to move your child up the ladder one rung at a time to increasingly more mature ways of expressing anger. Here are some guidelines that may help in that process:

First, *set the proper example.*

If you're constantly screaming obscenities or throwing things around the house in anger, you're going to have a hard time explaining to your children how to express anger appropriately.

POSITIVE
1. Pleasant • Seeking resolution • Focusing anger on source • Holding to primary complaint • Thinking logically
2. Pleasant • Focusing anger on source • Holding to primary complaint • Thinking logically

POSITIVE AND NEGATIVE
3. Focusing anger on source • Holding to primary complaint • Thinking logically • Unpleasant, loud
4. Holding to primary complaint • Thinking logically • Unpleasant, loud • Displacing anger to other sources
5. Focusing anger on source • Holding to primary complaint • Thinking logically • Unpleasant, loud • Verbal abuse
6. Holding to primary complaint • Thinking logically • Unpleasant, loud • Displacing anger to other sources
7. Thinking logically • Unpleasant, loud • Displacing anger to other sources • Expressing unrelated complaints

PRIMARILY NEGATIVE
8. Unpleasant, loud • Displacing anger to other sources • Expressing unrelated complaints • Emotionally destructive behavior
9. Unpleasant, loud • Displacing anger to other sources • Expressing unrelated complaints • Verbal abuse • Emotionally destructive behavior
10. Unpleasant, loud • Cursing • Displacing anger to other sources • Expressing unrelated complaints • Verbal abuse • Emotionally destructive behavior
11. Focusing anger on source • Unpleasant, loud • Cursing • Throwing objects • Emotionally destructive behavior
12. Unpleasant, loud • Cursing • Displacing anger to other sources • Throwing objects • Emotionally destructive behavior

NEGATIVE
13. Focusing anger on source • Unpleasant, loud • Cursing • Destroying property • Verbal abuse • Emotionally destructive behavior
14. Unpleasant, loud • Cursing • Displacing anger to other sources • Destroying property • Verbal abuse • Emotionally destructive behavior
15. Unpleasant, loud • Cursing • Displacing anger to other sources • Destroying property • Verbal abuse • Physical abuse • Emotionally destructive behavior
16. Passive-aggressive behavior

"The list of 15 ways of behaving while angry are combined in various arrangements on the Anger Ladder. Notice that most expressions of anger are primarily negative. On the ladder, only the top two rungs are totally positive. Each rung on the ladder represents a progressively better way to express anger. You want to train your child to take one step at a time, to go up one rung at a time."[6]

And if you respond to inappropriate anger with inappropriate anger, you'll only reinforce the pattern. But if your children see *you* learning to express your anger in a responsible and loving way, they'll have a model of hope to follow. (See "Learn the Art of Self-Control," below.)

Second, *train your kids to move toward more appropriate ways of expressing anger.*

The best way to accomplish that is by praising your child for whatever appropriate means he is using to express his anger, and by challenging him to correct one of the inappropriate ways he is expressing anger. Don't try to communicate either of those thoughts during the raging storm of anger, though; wait until the calm after the storm. Make sure that you challenge your child in bite-size chunks, and praise any progress lavishly.

Third, *recognize that your options are limited.*

You have only three options, really. You can work to allow your kids to find a proper way to express anger, you can let them express their anger in any way they choose, appropriate or inappropriate, or you can refuse to let them express their anger. Allowing the expression of anger and training for improvement will move your kids up the ladder toward increasingly mature behavior. Denying any expression of anger will most surely lead to some destructive expression of anger. You may temporarily save yourself a lot of confrontational grief, but that grief may be visited on you tenfold later in life, affecting not only your family but your extended family far into the future.

If you read Ross Campbell's book for the chapter on anger alone, it will be well worth the price. Here's one last quote from *How to Really Love Your Teenager:*

> Scripture instructs us to train a child in the way he should go. Forcing a child to suppress the anger and not to deal with it properly is training him in the way he should not go. It is crucial to train a child in the proper way to handle anger. This is done by teaching him to resolve the anger, not to suppress it.[7]

Allowing the expression of anger will go a long way toward keeping the doors of communication open during the difficult teen years.

Learn the Art of Self-Control

It isn't only our children's anger we need to be concerned with; make sure you express your *own* anger in appropriate ways as you communicate with your children. It's especially important that we not, in anger, say things to our kids that we don't really mean. A raised voice isn't likely to damage a child—unless you've been careless in choosing the words you express in that voice.

"Sticks and stones may break my bones, but names will never hurt me." Oh, yeah! Tell that to the little boy with glasses who is called "four eyes" by his new classmates. The person who came up with that maxim had a stone for a heart. And if that person is reading this, he, too, probably feels hurt or angry because of what I just said. The outer bruises caused by sticks and stones heal much faster than the bruises inflicted on the heart, and one of the reasons it's so important to have your own act together is so you can avoid the long-lasting damage that can be done when you lose control. I have counseled hundreds of wounded teenagers with scars branded on their hearts from words said by a parent in an uncontrolled moment, words those parents wish they could take back. Words like:

"I wish you'd never been born!"

"Get out of my sight—you make me sick."

"You're nothing but a slut!"

"You'll never amount to anything."

"You're so stupid!"

"I hate you when you're like this."

"You're a loser!"

In a moment of frustration and anger, those words can be out of your mouth before you know it. That's why, when you sense that you're losing control, it's so important to cool off before you continue. Call a time-out. Take as many time-outs as you need in order to keep the exchange rational.

Once the damaging words are out of your mouth, they can never be called back. If you want to keep the lines of communication open with your child, learn to keep yourself under control.

Don't Give Up

A parent has only so much energy. The exact amount of that energy is not measured in ergs or candle power; it is measured only in comparison with the energy of their children. Here's the formula: Count up all your kids, add together the amount of energy they have. You have less than that.

Keeping the lines of communication open with your kids will require all of that energy and then some, plus a generous helping of patience. There are days, as every parent knows, when it just doesn't seem worth the effort—especially as your kids approach adolescence. I want to encourage you that, with God's help (he has enough strength and energy for all of us), you *can make it*. Please don't give up.

Don't give up when they stop talking.

Teenagers are not generous with their communication. Their new-found independence and the increasing importance of their friends put you and me far down the communication priority list. Even well-established lines of parent-child communication will be strained by adolescence. It's tempting during this time to retreat to the safety of informational nagging and neglect deeper levels of communication where we feel more vulnerable. But the sad truth is that now, when your kids are most difficult to talk with, is when they need that deeper communication the most. And when their clumsy attempts at deeper communication are met with nagging questions and negative responses from a worried, confused, sometimes angry parent, hope soon fades, and they retreat into sullen silence. Don't give up.

Don't give up because your stomach is doing the Mexican hat dance.

You and your child will not be able to agree on everything, nor will you be able to resolve all your differences. Accept that fact—and keep talking. My kids and I have an agreement. We will not let each other give up on communication. I used to give up when the going got tough. When our disagreements reached a certain level of intensity, I would send the kids to their room or throw my hands up in desperation and walk away. Yet when they copied my behavior by stomping from the room with "You just don't understand," I would respond with anger. The doors to effective communication were closing quickly. Now, by mutual consent, we keep talking until we either agree or agree to disagree.

Don't send your kids from the room or leave the room yourself just to avoid an ulcer. Yes, there are times when you need to cool off before you can talk, but isolation should never take the place of communication. If a cooling-off period is needed, set a time for continuing the discussion—perhaps in an hour, or even the next day. Confrontation can be painful, but don't give up. Open communication is not only a two-way street, it's also a very broad street. It must be open to the high-speed, high-power traffic of conflict as well as the benign, Sunday-driver exchange of pleasantries.

Don't give up when you get no positive feedback.

"Talking to my kid is like talking to a wall."

"Whatever I say to my daughter just goes in one ear and out the other."

"Why bother trying to tell them anything? They don't hear a word that I say."

I can't count the times I've heard expressions like those, and more often than not I've heard them from my own lips. When you're giving it everything you've got, and there's no hint of response from your kids, you may wonder if it's worth the effort.

It is. A woman suddenly awoke from a coma that had lasted two months. During that time, her husband had spent every possible minute at her bedside. He held her hand and declared his love for her, even though he was getting nothing in return. There was no indication that his wife could hear him. Yet, when she woke, she was able to report that she had heard it all. During those months, his words of love and encouragement helped her fight her way back to consciousness.

Communicating with kids, especially teenagers, is not unlike talking to someone in a coma. But don't stop. They're hearing every word. Especially those level-three words that communicate love and encouragement. Someday they'll snap into a higher level of maturity and awareness and remember everything you said.

A runaway teenager in Los Angeles was headed for disaster. Out of money and desperate for food, she was on the shadowy edge of a life of prostitution. Terrified by the direction her life was heading, one night she picked up the phone and called her parents. Her life was saved by that phone call. When I asked her what gave her the courage to call she said, "I cheated and lied to my parents for two years before I ran away from home. Mom would try so hard to get through to me, but I treated her like dirt. Almost every day, my mother would say, 'There is nothing you can do to make me stop loving you.' I never gave her the satisfaction of knowing that her words were getting through. But after I ran away, I would hear those words in every quiet moment. And after I'd been beaten senseless by a man who wanted to be my pimp, I was lying in a filthy alley, ashamed and beyond hope. I'd been drugged, I'd been beaten, and just one thought kept running through my head: *There is nothing you can do to make me stop loving you.* I picked up the phone and called my mom. I had given up on myself, but I knew she hadn't given up on me."

Communication is so important to family relationships that it should be guarded like gold. If the lines become frayed for any amount of time, get help. Rebuilding lines that have been totally broken is a difficult and time-consuming task. Don't let things get that far; seek help from your pastor or a professional counselor, and mend the lines while they can still be used.

Keep the lines open even at great expense, of both time and money. Communication lines are lifelines. Sometimes the going will get tough—but don't give up.

5

Discipline Is Not a Dirty Word

A Case for Daring to Discipline

Discipline: Training that corrects, molds, or perfects. To train and develop by instruction and exercise especially in self control.[1]

I f it weren't for discipline, parenting wouldn't be too bad. Most parents have felt that way at one time or another. But the truth is, if it weren't for discipline, life would be impossible. Especially family life.

Discipline is the aspect of parenting that causes most prospective parents to tremble in fear. In forty-five years of life on earth, I've never met a parent who looked forward to the responsibility of discipline. Kids don't exactly relish it either. Throughout the ages, the cry "There are too many rules around here!" has been repeated a million times. It's been heard in caves, suburban homes, farmhouses, and primitive huts around the world. Little do the kids who bellow those declarations know what a world without rules would be like.

Although it's true that much of the conflict between parents and their kids revolves around discipline, that discipline is absolutely necessary for survival. Just watch the chaos and conflict in a home that has no rules, and you'll quickly recognize its value. Better yet, observe the self-doubt, fear, and immaturity in the life of a child who has had no rules.

In the fifties, a well-meaning group of people began a permissive movement that became a national disaster. Well-known doctors and pop psychologists suggested that children were somehow stifled and damaged by disciplinary actions. These people felt that, if left to themselves, kids would develop their own disciplinary guidelines. Dr. Benjamin Spock was probably the most visible spokesperson for this point of view. It was a bold experiment—but it didn't work. That permissive atmosphere led to a generation of anxious, insecure, and sometimes antisocial children who grew into anxious, insecure, and sometimes antisocial adults. The result of permissive parenting is not the utopia that Spock and others envisioned. The violent social chaos depicted in *Lord of the Flies* is closer to the truth.

In the decades since then, it has been demonstrated over and over that a lack of consistent, fair discipline in a child's life leads to disaster. Yet a large number of very visible people still try to promote the philosophy of permissive parenting. In his book *How to Make Your Child a Winner*, Dr. Victor Cline contrasted what he calls *permissiveness* or *family democracy* with a more direct approach to discipline, which he called *authoritarian*. While his book effectively demonstrates the emotional bankruptcy that results when a child is deprived of effective discipline, I believe that "family democracy," within the framework of consistent discipline, is a very good thing. Flexibility adds power to discipline, rather than weakening it. Why not incorporate the best of both philosophies—and, as much as possible, avoid their pitfalls? As Dr. James Dobson says in *Dare to Discipline:*

> Methods and philosophies regarding control of children have been the subject of heated debate and disagreement for centuries. The pendulum has swept back and forth regularly between harsh, oppressive discipline and the unstructured permissiveness of the 1950s. It is time that we realize that both extremes leave their characteristic scars on the lives of young victims, and I would be hard pressed to say which is more damaging.[2]

Discipline Isn't a Choice Between Two Extremes

In my seminars, participants often extol the virtues of either *authoritarian* or *permissive* parenting as if those two extremes were the only options. We'd have little hope for the welfare of our children if that were true, because either extreme will fail.

Total permissiveness will fail because kids have neither the experience, the wisdom, nor the moral superstructure to be able to cope with the complexities of life on their own. Kids need structure, and that structure includes discipline. One of the failed educational experiments of the past couple of decades was the attempt to remove walls from classrooms and guidelines from curriculum—elementary education with neither structure nor discipline. Educators expected to raise up a new generation of creative, unstifled children. That generation never materialized. What we discovered instead is that, with rare exceptions, kids work better within established, accepted structure, including properly administered disciplinary guidelines. That structure gives them confidence and a sense of security that stimulate, rather than stifle, creativity.

But here's the problem: Just because the philosophy of permissiveness, taken to its extremes, didn't work is not sufficient reason for parents to reject all of its parts. We should not, in reaction, swing to the other extreme and accept as the only option an unyielding, inflexible authoritarian approach to parenting and education. There is great value, for instance, in giving even a young child some power in choosing the content and direction of his education. One benefit of the "Era of Permissiveness" is that we laid to rest the old misguided adage, "Kids should be seen and not heard." Extreme authoritarianism is as dangerous and as much to be avoided as extreme permissiveness.

The next chapter will discuss the importance of *balance* in the administration of discipline. Balance is exactly what is needed here: the proper balance of reasonable authority and intelligent permissiveness that most effectively meets the needs of a growing child and concerned parent.

Discipline Is a Foundation for Growth

Consistent, loving discipline will give your kids two essential elements for a healthy journey to adulthood.

First, *it gives them the emotional freedom to move toward independence with safety and confidence.*

When I first learned to fly, my instructor told me to never go near the clouds. That was the most ridiculous thing I'd ever heard. Why would my instructor want to place such a dumb restriction on my freedom? One of the main reasons I was learning to fly was so that I could play in the clouds!

"Why *can't* I go near the clouds?" I whined.

My instructor's answer didn't make sense. If I went into a cloud without the proper training, he said, I wouldn't be able to tell whether I was upside down or right side up. "You can lose control of the airplane and die," he said.

Who was he trying to kid? I was certainly old enough to know which end of my body was up. I had only been turned upside down a couple of times in my life, but each time I'd been very much aware of it. I decided that the rules didn't apply to me.

Shortly after getting my license, I rented a plane and went cloud hunting. I found a cloud about the size of a house and looked it over. *What danger could possibly be lurking in a baby cloud?* I scoffed. With a delicious sense of fear and excitement, I broke the rule—I flew into the cloud. It was marvelous! The world of living color disappeared in total whiteness, only to suddenly reappear brighter than ever. When I came out, I looked around the cockpit. *As I suspected!* Everything was right side up.

Braver now, I found a huge billowing cloud. *If a small cloud was fun*, I reasoned, *then surely a big cloud will be funner!* I inspected the marshmallow edges of this monster, then cautiously snuggled up close enough to stick a wing in the cloud. When I pulled the wing out—*it was still right side up!* Filled with confidence, I circled, made a run at the cloud, and dove in!

Inside, it was like a roller coaster. One second I was light as a feather, my stomach sharing the same space as my Adam's

apple, and the next my body was pressed deep into the seat. Suddenly, the most amazing thing happened: All the books and pencils in the airplane floated to about eye level and hovered there momentarily before being snapped to the ceiling as though drawn by a powerful magnet. *So that's why they tell you not to fly in clouds,* I concluded. *They want to keep you from enjoying this wonderful secret!*

The same moment that thought entered my mind, the plane exited the clouds—*upside down* and spinning out of control. First, I froze in terror—then I called on all I'd learned in my months of training, let go of the control wheel, and screamed for my mommy. God must have had a guardian angel with me that day, because the plane righted itself just enough that I could bring it under control. Shaking like a leaf, I headed back to the airport. After landing and leaving my lunch on the parking ramp, I went straight to the flight office and signed up to learn to fly by instrument rules.

Talk about discipline! Instrument rules fill several books. Why would I want to subject myself to such discipline after, shortly before, wanting to ignore much simpler discipline? Why? Because my terrifying brush with disaster had reminded me of an important truth: Although rules may cramp my style and keep me from exploring every option life has to offer, they actually protect my life and give me freedom that I could never enjoy without them. By following the very strict rules of instrument flying, I can take off from Denver, enter the clouds at 200 feet, fly 500 miles without seeing the ground, and pop out of the clouds (right side up) with the runway of my choice right in front of the plane. If I choose to disobey the rules, I'll quickly get lost and will jeopardize my life. More pilots die every year because they refuse to obey the rules of flying than from any other cause.

Asking our kids to walk through life without the guidelines of discipline is like asking them to fly through the clouds without instruments. We might as well hand them a death warrant. Giving kids the advantage of disciplinary guidelines literally sets them free. Someone summarized it best in this phrase: "He who is enslaved to the compass has the freedom of the seas." The guidelines and rules of discipline give kids the compass they need to negotiate a stormy world. Rather than fearfully stumbling about without boundaries, they can run, confident and free, within the boundaries. Without discipline, kids get lost; some completely lose their bearing, turn upside down, and die.

Privileged Information, a newsletter published by Boardroom Reports, Inc., states in its December 15, 1991, issue:

> Strong direction and support—not freedom—are what nurture high-achieving and confident children, concludes a researcher with the Institute of Human Development, University of California at Berkeley. The recent study found that "Children who grow up with high control and high support are more confident and better achievers than those raised with high support and low control (or with low support and high control, or with low support and low control)."

Discipline Is a Confirmation of Love

The second element discipline brings to your child's life is: *It confirms your love.*

Your kids may kick and scream, as most do, about anything that even hints at discipline; yet inwardly they interpret that discipline as evidence of your love. There are many signs kids watch for to confirm that they are loved. Discipline is one of the most important. I've never met a child without discipline who felt secure and loved.

In *How to Live With Your Parents Without Losing Your Mind*, I told the story of a young boy who was in constant trouble with the law. This boy forged elaborate permission slips allowing him to go on three consecutive weeks of canoe trips. As leader of the canoe trips, I became suspicious, and paid a visit to his mother—only to discover that she had not known where he was, nor did she care. She was just glad to have him out of the house.

I confronted him. "Why," I asked, "did you bother to forge the notes? Your mother would have let you go anyway!"

It was the only time I saw this rebellious and angry young man soften. Holding back the tears, he answered, "I wanted you to think somebody cared." The notes he had forged were written with the kind of parental concern that usually embarrasses and angers a child. Unable to produce genuine evidence of a mother who cared, he pretended; he forged notes filled with that evidence.

---

*He who is enslaved to the compass
has the freedom of the seas.*

I have worked with hundreds of kids like that young man. On the outside, they wear a mask of bravado and rebellion to cover an inside of loneliness, insecurity, and fear. The strongest evidence that discipline is a sign of love comes from observing broken-hearted kids who had parents who didn't care enough to discipline.

But you do care. That's why you bought this book. So why would I take up this space reminding you of the importance of discipline? Because it's a frustrating hassle to establish rules and guidelines and then have to enforce them. If you're like me, you're often tempted to throw in the towel. If it's so clear that our kids need discipline, why is discipline such a hassle? For one simple reason: *They don't know it!*

To a teenager, "He who is enslaved to the compass is a *slave.*" Period. They don't see the freedom that comes from rules, only the restrictions. So they kick and fight any attempt to establish a new rule, and after the rule has been established, they test it. By testing your rule, they are also testing your resolve—and your love.

Don't be discouraged. Rule-testing is part of the job description of a kid. Even small children do it. In airports across the country, I often see little kids tethered to a parent by a telephone-cord-type leash designed to keep them from wandering off. I have yet to see a kid walking close to his parent with the cord slack. They're always way out at the end, stretching the cord to the breaking point, dragging a haggard parent whose nerves are as stretched as the cord.

Teenagers are worse; they're like the horses we used to raise. We had three horses and three hundred and fifty acres of lush pasture for them to roam. Yet they were always pressed up against the fence with their necks stretched to the limit to nibble some dust-covered bit of grass *outside* the pasture.

When your kid is stamping around the house, slamming doors and throwing a fit because of some restriction on her behavior, when you are standing toe-to-toe with the fruit of your loins and the veins in your neck are bigger than his legs, when you have carefully explained the reasons for your actions and you get that look usually reserved for insects—then you'll be tempted, as I am, to throw your arms in the air and say, "Who needs this!" This chapter was written to remind you: Your kids need it.

There are few responsibilities in life as physically and emotionally draining as the responsibility to provide discipline. There are even fewer responsibilities that will give your kids a more solid foundation for growth and development. It *is* worth the effort. Life without discipline would be like a game without rules—confusing, shapeless, and you'd never even know if you were winning. Discipline is hard evidence of your love. It will save untold heartache in the future, and it will give you a yardstick by which you and your children can measure progress.

Now, if you bought all that, I have a tightrope to sell you. And you'd better take it, because you're going to need it. As we'll discuss in the next chapter, providing consistent, loving discipline is a balancing act worthy of headline billing in a circus.

6

Walking the Tightrope

*The Balancing Act of Consistent,
Loving Discipline*

G ood discipline, as chapter 5 explained, requires balancing permissiveness and authority. It also requires a
delicate balance of skills to make it to the other side of
parenthood with your body and mind intact (well, okay—just
your body).

The key word is *balance*. Every action a parent takes is most
effective when it is balanced with another action. And that's
not easy—it requires thought, consideration for the feelings of
your child, and a tremendous amount of self-control. Fortunately, the rewards for all that effort go beyond positively
influencing your child's growth. It is also rewarding to see your
own continued growth as a parent as you begin to experience
some measure of control—both of yourself and of your
relationship with your son or daughter.

When we feel defeated by parenting, one of the reasons is
that our parenting decisions are often not decisions at all—
they're simply reactions to a stimulus, and the stimulus is
whatever happens to be the crisis of the moment. Our children
behave inconsiderately, and we react out of the pain their
behavior causes to our ego and out of the context of the high-
pressure lives we lead. Those quick and careless reactions,
besides doing little or no good for our children, cause us to feel

dry, out of control, and guilty. It would be better, for both you and your children, to offer them a thought-out response designed to demonstrate the love of Christ and build their character.

Is it possible to break that destructive pattern of negative stimulus/angry response? Yes. But to do that, you'll have to take advantage of the lull between the storms to form a balanced plan of action, based on the suggestions in the rest of this chapter. Then you'll be better prepared to respond calmly and wisely, rather than simply reacting blindly—next time your son comes home with his nose pierced or your daughter gets picked up for shoplifting.

Balance Discipline With Love

Effectively balancing discipline and love is one of the keys to raising healthy kids. How are we parents to maintain that difficult balance? By making unconditional love the bedrock foundation of our discipline. Yes, *you* know that you love your kids even when you punish them—but it's critical that you let *them* know it. When a small child receives a deserved spanking or a teenager is denied a privilege, it should be parenthesized with reassuring hugs or verbal expressions of love. Older children, especially, may be too angry to let you touch them immediately after disciplining. But that shouldn't stop you from saying those three magic words. They may not soothe your child's immediate anger, but they'll be heard—and not forgotten.

Withholding your expressions of love should never be used as a disciplinary measure. When I was a child (my kids think that was shortly before dinosaurs became extinct), such behavior was called coddling and was thought to nullify the effect of discipline. Parents of that period felt that any display of affection so close to discipline would spoil the child. Many still believe that. But I have counseled many kids who've spent days and sometimes weeks without expressions of love from parents who were withholding their love as a form of punishment. These well-meaning parents were trying to emphasize the undesirability of a particular behavior. Instead, it was the children who felt undesirable. These kids reasoned: "Mom and Dad only love me when I'm good. Since I can never be good enough to perfectly please them, they must not love me."

Think I'm exaggerating? Just check with the counselors who have struggled to help get the lives of those who were denied love as children back on track. Many of these unfortunate people—and they tend to be self-deprecating over-achievers—have no self-esteem, because they learned as children that self-esteem is based on ability to perform up to expectations.

Withholding love should never be a form of discipline.

Recently I overheard a man criticize his daughter for affectionately cuddling her children after discipline. "If you do that," he said, "you're teaching them that you love them even when they misbehave."

I wanted to shout, "*Yes!* That's the whole idea!" That man believed, obviously, that expressing love after discipline encourages the bad behavior. He was wrong. You can make it very clear that you are upset with the bad behavior but that you still love your child. The proper balance of administering discipline and expressing love teaches your kids that your love is unconditional, that you love them even when they are bad. Balance your discipline with large doses of physical and verbal expressions of love.

Balance Control and Cooperation

Allow your kids to help set rules and determine proper discipline; it will help them learn sound judgment and understand the principles behind the rules.

Periodically, we have a family forum to review the guidelines that have been set for each child. Our kids are encouraged to be more than grumblers and whiners in these meetings; we invite them to participate fully. Where they have demonstrated maturity, we are open to relaxing some of the existing rules.

Where they have been disobedient, the rules are occasionally tightened. And it's Taryn and Traci, as much as Diane and I, who determine whether relaxing or tightening is needed.

These meetings also give us the chance to identify new areas of responsibility and to establish guidelines for those areas. Taryn and Traci have the opportunity at these meetings to express their frustration over current rules and to point out areas where Diane and I can be more flexible. As you might imagine, sometimes the discussion gets heated. But I've been amazed by the peace in our family in the days that follow. Because they have been involved in the process, the kids seem willing to follow the rules with less rebellion. Even the rules they feel are too strict produce less anger because the girls understand the principles behind them.

If you decide to institute meetings of this type in your own family, remember that it's important to keep a cool head while your kids are pushing—sometimes impatiently—for every freedom they can negotiate. Losing control of your own emotions can shut down that open flow of communication so vital to the process. And remember: This is not the time to dispense discipline or to reprimand your kids for bad behavior. This is the time to work together with your spouse and kids to create the framework for discipline.

How do you maintain balance in these meetings? By establishing from the beginning that you are willing to listen to all suggestions but that you are responsible for making the final decisions. If you're flexible enough to respond to their concerns, you'll be amazed at the difference in their attitude. Even though the final decision is yours, your kids will feel, because of the process of discussion and mutual listening during the meetings, that you respect them and that you're genuinely concerned with their feelings.

The decisions you make in these sessions should be reviewed three or four times a year. Kids are constantly entering new arenas, such as driving and dating, for which new responsibilities and guidelines must be considered. You can often avoid misunderstandings and problems by deciding ahead of time what guidelines will govern these areas, rather than waiting until a problem develops.

I am amazed at how these meetings motivate my children to prove their maturity. A few months ago, my daughter Traci was spending so much time on the phone I was afraid she was going to end up with a cauliflower ear and I was going to develop a gastric ulcer. Almost all her waking hours were spent with Ma Bell. Those of you with newborn children, be forewarned: Shortly after the umbilical cord is cut, it is replaced with a telephone cord.

**Bad behavior should never be a
reward for good behavior.**

I told Traci that her behavior demonstrated a poor use of her time and pushed her privileges way past the limit. I was also disappointed by her insensitivity to my obvious distress over her behavior. She argued that as long as she was getting good grades and keeping up with her chores, she should be able to talk on the phone as long as she wanted. My parental red flag went up at that point because I strongly believe that bad behavior should never be a reward for good behavior.

So I threatened to set a time limit, which is sometimes the only way to resolve such conflicts. But Traci strongly resisted the idea of a time limit because, as she explained it, many times her friends called with problems. How could she just hang up in the middle of helping a hurting friend simply because the time limit was up? I respected that reasoning, but I also knew that most of the calls from Traci's friends were not emergencies; her long hours on the phone consisted mostly of idle conversation punctuated by long periods of silence. To a teenager, any ringing phone is an emergency.

After a long, sometimes heated discussion clarifying our positions, it was my duty to make a decision. We agreed that Traci would have two weeks to demonstrate that she could handle the phone responsibly without restriction. If there was a genuine crisis, she was to let me know and I would exercise benevolent flexibility. On all other occasions, she was to limit her phone calls to a reasonable amount of time. If I was uncomfortable with the amount of time she had been on the phone, I would signal my distress (clutching at my heart and drooling with my eyes rolled back in my head), and she would terminate that call at the first appropriate moment. "Appropriate," of course, is a vague term, and we agreed that Traci would be responsible for determining what amount of time was appropriate. (Remember that our discussion had been thorough enough that she knew my feelings.)

Traci listened to my decision and agreed to give it a try, even though she made it clear that she felt my expectations were way too strict. If you're a fairly strict parent, you may feel that my decision was too lenient. But I made that decision because of my belief in the principle that teenagers learn more from the opportunity to set their own rules—where that freedom is safe and practical—rather than living according to hard and fast rules made by their parents. In a few years, young adulthood will force them to make such decisions. Why not give them a head start learning those skills?

Six months have passed since that conversation, and I have been astounded at the way Traci has handled her responsibility. There hasn't been a single crisis requiring a marathon conversation, and she has been sensitive to the few times I have clutched my heart and drooled all over her carpet to express my concern over the length of a call. Even better, she is doing all this with an excellent attitude. Is she on the phone more than I would like? Yes! (Anything over thirty seconds is more than I would like.) But she's demonstrating responsible restraints. And there is peace where once only battles raged.

Respect begets respect.

If she had continued to be irresponsible, I would have set a specific limit on her phone use until she demonstrated the ability to make good judgments on her own. But I refuse to make a rule just to avoid the conflict of working it out together.

Cooperating with your kids doesn't require that you relinquish your role as a parent. Even as you cooperate, never lose sight of the fact that *you* are the one responsible for the final decision. The attempt to cooperate with your kids should not become an opportunity for your kids to control you. Instead, it's an opportunity for you to exercise positive control in the maturing process of your children. Relinquishing your role as a parent isn't cooperation; it's abandonment—and abdication of your responsibility in the lives of your kids. On the other hand, don't make the mistake of thinking that a willingness to listen and be flexible is a sign of weakness. The secret is balance.

The positive aspects of working together are too great to ignore. Cooperation allows your kids to see the connection between your expectations and the principles they spring from. It motivates them to make responsible decisions on their own—a strategic skill they will sorely need when they leave your influence. Cooperation makes your kids feel loved by showing that you are concerned about their feelings and willing to be flexible where possible. It gives you the opportunity to see their growing maturity and to reward it with more responsibility. It gives them a chance to respond to you with more than just angry, rebellious compliance.

These are great benefits. Balancing cooperation and control is definitely worth the effort.

Balance Privacy With Perceptiveness

It is impossible to discipline your child unless you know what is going on in his or her life. Especially during the early adolescent years, when kids suddenly become intensely private, they can make that very difficult. You must keep your eyes and ears wide open to gather as much information as possible.

This parental need for information gathering runs headlong into another need that is just as important: your child's need for privacy. That need is so important that adolescents will stop just short of killing a sibling for invading that privacy. Since a certain amount of privacy is a natural component of adolescents' expression of independence, how far should you go to find out what's happening inside their head—or what problems and temptations they're facing when they're out of your sight?

Once again, balance is the key. If the communication lines are open and you are taking the time to listen, then your children will feel the freedom to convey much of that information to you. And excessive prying into every detail of their lives robs your children of precious privacy that they need. But just because a little privacy is good, it doesn't necessarily follow that a whole lot is better. Total secrecy between adolescent and parent is a dangerous invitation to trouble.

Let them control their part of the beach, but don't bury your head in the sand.

I'm always amused by the signs that appear on the bedroom doors of adolescent children. "Enter at your own risk!" "A killer cat protects this room!" Recently I stayed at a home in Canada where the following hand-printed sign guarded the privacy of a young lady's room:

Do not enter without knocking. If there is no answer just try later or contact me another way.

Kari Olson

On my daughter's door I found this sign:

Room rules:

Admittance by invitation only. Anyone with food has an open invitation. Good-looking men are always welcome. Brothers are never welcome (except in life-and-death situations). Do not straighten anything. Telephone is for emergencies only. (All my calls are emergencies.) This is a nagging-free zone.

We should expect these requests for privacy, and we should honor them. Yet in order to fulfill our duties as parents, we should also have access to our children's rooms. And when you enter those rooms, keep your eyes wide open; those rooms hold many secrets about what is going on in their owners' lives. The walls alone speak volumes. My younger daughter's room is plastered with posters of animals: a gorilla holding a kitten, a baby giraffe, two puppies in a sewing basket. My favorite shows an obese puppy sitting on a scale. The caption reads, "O Lord help me, for I am in trouble."

My older daughter's room no longer holds animal pictures. Kirk Cameron, the wholesome and handsome star of the popular television show "Growing Pains," has the most prominent place on her wall. Pictures of her friends are scattered everywhere. There is a romantic picture of a couple walking hand in hand, and there's even a large picture of her wholesome and handsome father clinging to a spot on her bulletin board. Seeing all of this helps me understand what changes are taking place in my girls' lives, and what's going on inside their heads. For my youngest daughter, anything with more than two legs is at the top of her interest list, and her room shows it. My oldest daughter focuses on animals of the two-legged variety, and her room shows it.

I have lost count of the parents who watched their kids' rooms slowly fill with pictures of negative role models, heavy-metal rock stars, sexually suggestive posters, macabre skulls, and occult symbols, only to discover too late that it was more than just a passing fad. It was evidence of some serious changes in the attitudes of their children. I don't believe that a parent should search a kid's room or read a diary unless there is a *serious* reason. (Strong evidence that your child is involved in drugs or the occult, or suspicion that your child is experiencing depression bordering on suicide, are examples of reasons I would consider adequate for the extreme step of infringing on your child's privacy.) But I also don't believe a parent should enter a kid's room with eyes closed. Most kids are pretty careless. It isn't only dirty clothing, candy wrappers, and paper they leave strewn about; they also leave cigarettes, pornography, drug paraphernalia, and notes.

Don't ignore your child's room as a potential source for understanding the strengths and weaknesses of your child. But observe a simple courtesy in doing so: Knock before entering.

The older your children are, the more important this simple expression of respect becomes.

Establish, so that every member of your family understands it, that you as parent have the right to enter your child's room to bring in fresh clothing (or a bulldozer if the room needs it), investigate noxious odors, and so on. And once you're in, keep your eyes open. I have an agreement with my children that I will never read their journal unless I fear for their life. But any note or scrap of paper that clutters their room is fair game. Never have I scoured their rooms for those notes, but by simply keeping my eyes open I have discovered information that has helped head off trouble—and I've never yet been accused of destroying their privacy.

There's an old saying that your sins will find you out. Kids often leave tangible evidence of their sins where alert parents can't miss them. Traci is convinced that God has a tattletale guardian angel assigned to her. One day shortly after she entered junior high, she left a note written to a friend in plain view on *my* desk. As I set it aside, a single phrase caught my eye: "Sally sure got drunk last night. Pretty cool, huh!"

Time for a conference. When she got home from school, I asked, "Traci, does Sally drink?"

"No," she quickly answered, avoiding eye contact.

I gave her one more chance. "Look at me, Traci, and tell me whether Sally drinks."

"No, Dad," she said as her eyes grew wide and her face grew red.

"Then what is this?" I asked, handing her the note. The color that had just moved into her face drained away. She stared at the note for what seemed an eternity. Then her face crumpled and the tears began to flow. The discussion that followed was painful, very revealing, and worth every minute. I discovered that Traci was at a very vulnerable point in her life, facing peer pressures she'd never had to face in grade school. Although she didn't drink, she had adopted a tolerant attitude toward drinking because so many of her friends did it. She had lied to me because she was afraid that if I knew her friend drank, I wouldn't let Traci associate with her.

This teachable moment gave me the chance to address

several critical issues before they exploded into big problems. We talked again about how lying destroys trust. We also talked about the need to take a stand. I explained that if she demonstrated the maturity to take a stand on these issues, I would have little fear of her friendship with kids who had different values. I also expressed my desire that she choose most of her friends from among kids who held similar values to hers.

This confrontation came at a perfect time. But it would never have happened if I hadn't had my eyes open. I do not purposely read the notes of my children—but neither do I pretend not to see what her tattletale guardian angel puts on my desk.

A friend left home recently with explicit instructions for his eighteen-year-old daughter. She was responsible for her younger sister, and under no circumstances was she to leave her alone. But after the parents left, friends invited the older girl out, and she couldn't resist. She made her younger sister promise not to tell on her, to lock the doors, and not to leave the house. Then she left her sister alone with a supply of pizza and stepped out. She planned to be back in time to clean up any incriminating evidence. She covered all the bases except one: She forgot to take the keys to the house.

When she returned, her little sister had fallen asleep and didn't hear the doorbell or her pounding on the doors and windows. The neighbors, however, were not asleep, and did hear the ruckus. They called the police, thinking that a burglar was trying to get in.

When the parents came home, red lights from police cars were flashing everywhere. Almost as much light was coming from the very red face of their embarrassed daughter. The tattletale guardian angel had struck again.

God *is* on our side as parents. He helps us learn of impending problems before it's too late. Come to think of it, he does it because he's on the kids' side, too.

Give your kids the privacy they need, but keep your eyes and ears open so that you can take advantage of the teachable moments the angel brings to your attention.

Balance Being a Boss With Being a Buddy

This balance is absolutely necessary for a healthy parent-child relationship. Some experts teach that we should always be the boss and never play the role of buddy. Others suggest that your son or daughter should be your best friend. I think both extremes are unhealthy. Even though I'm a strong advocate of listening to kids and involving them in decision making, I believe just as strongly that your child should never be in doubt as to who is the boss.

Growing up, the times I felt my dad was my buddy were those rare and wonderful moments we spent hunting or fishing. I knew he was the boss; there was no doubt about that in our family. But for those magical moments, he was also my friend.

The problem is that one without the other gives a dangerous imbalance. If you make an attempt to be your child's best friend above everything else, you will relinquish your ability to be an effective parent, able to wield authority when needed. If you refuse to accept the role of friend on occasion, you relinquish the chance to show love in a special way and to stand close to your children in their unguarded moments. Most parents have no trouble playing the role of boss but find it difficult to take the time to be a friend. Yet it's such an important balance that its success affects every other balance discussed in this chapter. As Josh McDowell and Dick Day say in *How to Be a Hero to Your Kids*, "Rules without relationships leads to rebellion."

> Children do not respond to rules; they respond to relationships. It's true that you can get your children to "behave" by enforcing the rules. You can control your children to a certain point by running a tight ship, but that doesn't necessarily mean you are getting their loving and obedient response. What you are getting is their reaction, which may look like obedience on the surface, but beneath there is fear, frustration, and anger.
>
> Unless you establish a loving, accepting relationship with your child, you can almost count on trouble down the line. In fact, Scripture warns parents not to provoke or exasperate their children (See Ephesians 6:4, Colossians 3:32). . . . Rules with-

out relationships will almost always exasperate or provoke a child into negative behavior.[1]

This balance is beautifully demonstrated by my relationship with God. There is no doubt about his lordship in my life. I have purposely chosen to make him the boss. But I am also eternally grateful for those moments when he demonstrates the friendship side of his love. Because he is the boss, I feel free to look to him for direction and discipline. Because he is my friend, I can go to him when I hurt. He has never let me down in either role.

In our relationship with our children, this balance is best illustrated in an equation from *How to Be a Hero to Your Kids*:

RULES – A RELATIONSHIP = REBELLION
RULES + A RELATIONSHIP = RESPONSE[2]

Balance Punishment and Praise

Punishment is a method of teaching principle—not a tool for revenge. Keeping that in mind will often make it easier to decide what (and whether) punishment should be handed out. If you use punishment simply as a deterrent ("and if you ever do that again, you know what'll happen to you"), it will stop being effective when your kid figures out a way to keep you from finding out. But if it is used both as a deterrent and as a way to teach your child principles, the inner conviction that develops will stand even when the enforcer is not around.

Two overriding rules to keep in mind:

First, *punishment should always be carried out when you are under control*. The minute you find out that your thirteen-year-old son took the car for a joyride may not be the best time to decide the sentence. Twenty years of hard labor in a foreign country may seem entirely appropriate to you at that moment; an hour or two later, when you've cooled off, you'll probably realize that five years would be plenty.

With smaller children, it's often necessary to respond immediately, so that they can connect the punishment with the behavior. It's still important to keep control. A broken heirloom cookie jar may enrage you. But the child had no idea of the importance of the cookie jar. Express your displeasure about the sneaky action of stealing cookies, then wait until you've cooled down a bit about the cookie jar before taking action.

Second: *Avoid punishing older children (from about school age up) in front of friends if possible.* I have never met a child who didn't feel that a family trust was being violated by public punishment. I have also never met a child who didn't try at one time or other to get away with murder in the presence of others. Unless the child is clearly being manipulative, try to do your correction in private. If you're being manipulated, do your correction on the spot—and then make it clear that your action was necessitated by your child's manipulative behavior. Explain that you prefer not to do this in public but will if needed.

Another reason to avoid public punishment is that we parents can't always trust ourselves to maintain control over our emotions in that situation. We're often so embarrassed by our children's behavior and by how it reflects on us that the punishment can cease to be punishment for principles violated and become revenge for our embarrassment.

Balance the Punishment With the Crime

Make the punishment fit the crime. Reserve weeks of grounding for federal offenses. For a teenager, a weekend at home is like a year with an tax auditor for an adult. My teenage daughters consider a weekend away from their friends to be an almost unthinkable punishment. The whole world could be tortured to death slowly in a weekend. Those of us who have been around for thirty or more years think just the opposite: A year goes by like a weekend. Most parents and counselors agree that a weekend without social contact with friends is a punishment plenty traumatic to fit the offenses of most teens and preteen children. Some counselors argue that groundings of longer than a week are counterproductive, because kids can't see the light at the end of the tunnel. To them, it's like being grounded for the rest of your life. The result is that kids sneak out, willing to risk your wrath because things couldn't possibly get any worse than they are.

For smaller kids, half an hour can seem like a lifetime. Sitting in an airport, I heard the loudspeaker announce that boarding would begin in about twenty minutes. After about ten seconds, a boy of three years piped up, "Has twenty minutes started yet?" With an affirming hug, the boy's mom assured him that they would shortly be on their way to see grandma. The boy's next question touched off an explosion of laughter: "Will grandma still be alive in twenty minutes?"

My mother used to say, "I want you to stand in that corner for an hour, and I don't want to hear a peep out of you!" For the first three minutes, I would stand there making defiant little peeping noises. In the next two minutes, I would memorize every detail of the wall in front of me. If a spider happened along, I could last two or three more minutes, but beyond that I went crazy. Remember how a kid views time, and discipline accordingly.

Considering corporal punishment: I would slap the hand of my small child any day to save her life. I would rather see her learn from that small pain not to play with the light socket than see her electrocuted. During your child's earlier years, you can generally use that same method for disciplining outright disobedience and antisocial behavior. After all, if such behavior is ignored, the result can be just as devastating as sticking a nail file in a light socket. James Dobson has written an excellent book on this subject, *Dare to Discipline*. I highly recommend it.

In my endorsement of corporal punishment, I am not endorsing child abuse. Child abuse is an epidemic that must be battled on all fronts. But we must not be frightened away from loving discipline simply because it is sometimes confused with physical abuse. Neglecting to deal with behavioral problems that can lead to a ruined life is another form of child abuse that is just as inexcusable.

Disciplinary action and confrontation are usually seen as unpleasant and regrettable by both parent and child. Try to view them instead as valuable teaching opportunities.

The goal of disciplining your children is to one day see them value as their own some of the same principles that you have tested and learned to trust. When that happens, you'll see the source of control begin to shift (as it must) from parent-control to self-control.

And isn't that what the balancing act of consistent, loving discipline is all about?

7

Fertilizing Your Kids
The Art of Molding Character

T he inner character of a child often seems as untouchable
as the end of a rainbow. Perhaps that's because every
child has a unique character that exists apart from any efforts
to shape it. This fact is illustrated by a puzzle we've all
observed many times: Children of unloving, neglectful parents
sometimes grow up with a compassionate, loving character,
and children of caring, compassionate parents occasionally
grow up to be cruel and hateful. Despite this phenomenon,
there is much about a child's character we *can* shape and
mold. Unlike the end of a rainbow, you *can* touch the inner
character of your children.

In the end, of course, they will make the final decisions
about what kind of people they will be. But no one else in their
lives will have as great an opportunity as you to influence those
decisions. That is an awesome responsibility. But with God's
help and an awareness of the principles that influence
character, you can provide the foundation upon which your
child can choose to build a responsible and positive life.

In this chapter, we'll look at some guidelines to help you do
that. But first, a word of caution: You'll be setting yourself up
for deep disappointment if you envision the perfect character
for your child and then set out to get your son or daughter to

conform to that image. The character you envision simply may not match the personality God gave to that child. A much less frustrating approach is to use the guidelines in this chapter to provide the proper environment for character growth, and then model in your own life the characteristics that you wish for your child.

Understand the Importance of Rules

As I explained in the previous chapter, I believe that rules and their enforcement provide an important guidance system that frees kids to grow with security and confidence. But do rules help build character?

In one of my favorite stories, a little girl was misbehaving on a commercial airliner. She ran up and down the aisles disturbing the passengers until finally the stewardess brought her to her mother. "You need to keep your daughter seated," the stewardess insisted.

The mother roughly pushed the little girl into her seat, snapped the seatbelt tight around her, and hissed through clenched teeth, "Now you sit!"

The little girl obediently sat with her arms folded and an impish smile on her face.

"Why are you smiling?" the angry mother snapped.

"Because," the little girl smirked, "I may be sitting on the outside, but on the inside I'm still running around."

The seatbelt could only restrain her body; it couldn't change the little girl's heart. Don't miss the important lesson here: Changing the behavior of a child with rules will not *guarantee* a change of heart. But a changed heart will *always* result in changed behavior. Other than providing a stable environment from which character can spring, rules as an end in themselves do little to touch the character of a child. However, rules that are established and enforced in such a way as to teach principles can have a powerful effect on the development of character. Rules can give a child the chance to see the valuable principles behind certain kinds of behavior. Of course, it's better to have rules originate from an inner principle, but since few kids are born with a set of principles in place, rules can be used to come at the principle through the back door.

Assume, for instance, that your daughter doesn't like to study. I know, I know, that's hard to imagine—but bear with me. Assume that you insist that she spend a certain amount of time each day studying her schoolwork. Because you insist, she slowly begins to experience the benefits of study. She gets good grades, and because of that she gains certain privileges, both at home and at school. As she enters high school, she discovers that because of her grades she has a wide choice of colleges and the possibility of several scholarships. It's quite possible that, at some point in that process, without being consciously aware of it, your daughter will begin to personally value good study habits. Now she studies—not because you insist, but because it is one of her own principles for success. *She would never have experienced the benefits of study or established study as a personal value if she had not been forced to study in the first place.* Rules introduced her to principles that eventually became her own and that will serve her well. But the rules themselves were only a short-term solution; if she had not developed the personal value system that encouraged studying, this girl would have stopped studying as soon as she left the influence of her parents.

When setting rules, always tie the rule to the principle behind it. A small child told not to play in the street should be told that there's a reason for the rule—the pain that accompanies tire prints on their clothing.

Older kids, in particular, are fond of scoffing as you explain these principles: "Oh, come on, Dad! That's never going to happen!" Don't let that deter you. The old saying, "Rules are made to be broken," is true only if the rules become an end in themselves and are not tied to sound principles. If, on the other hand, the principles behind the rules are in clear focus, then rules can help build character.

Focus on the Principles

I grew up believing that a certain set of specific behaviors made a person a Christian. If you didn't smoke, drink, go to the theater, play cards, dance, or run around with people who did such things, you were a good Christian.

One day as I sat on the porch, Ralph, my collie dog, walked by. Suddenly it hit me. Ralph didn't smoke, drink, chew, go to the theater, dance, or play cards! And we never let Ralph run around with dogs that were involved in those things. Ralph, by the logic I was using, was a better Christian than I! The best Christians in the universe must be the mannequins you see in department stores—they don't do anything.

I have discovered since then that being a Christian is the result of an inside-and-out change of heart that comes from experiencing the personal forgiveness of Jesus Christ. That knowledge changed my perspective. Instead of reacting to the temptations of life by saying, *I can't do that because there's a rule against it*, I could now honestly say, *I don't want to do that because of the values I believe in*.

> The rules that can withstand all
> outside pressure are those
> that correspond with your
> child's inner commitment to principle.

Because rules do not emphasize principles, they work from the outside in. A child who depends on rules alone to guide his behavior, when asked by friends to take a drink, will respond by saying, "I can't. My parents would kill me." As with all outside motivation, there's a fatal flaw in this equation. If this child can be convinced that he won't get caught, he *will* take a drink. As soon as the outside pressure is removed (as soon as he's convinced that his parents won't find out and therefore *won't* kill him), there's nothing left to keep him from acting unwisely. Or if peer pressure reaches the point that it's stronger than your child's fear of your reprisal, he will give in.

Are there no rules that will stand, then? Yes. The rules that can withstand all outside pressure are those that correspond with your child's inner commitment to principle.

Our goal as parents, then, is not *just* to change our children's outward behavior; we also need to affect their inner commitment to principle, the values that govern the way they see themselves and the world. If we're successful in that, we effect change from the inside out. The child who has a personal commitment not to drink because of his personal value system will be strong in resisting outside pressure.

One day I sat down on a park bench to catch my breath after I finished jogging. I quickly realized that several boys were smoking marijuana in a cluster of bushes directly behind the bench. There was a lot of rough talk, and it smelled like they were burning their underwear.

"Come on, Dennis, take a hit," one of the boys urged.

"No thanks."

"Hey, come on—one hit's not gonna hurt you."

Dennis responded with an expletive that describes droppings from the male of the bovine species. "My brother walks around like a zombie because of that stuff, man."

Another voice this time. "Whatsa matter—you chicken?"

"Jeez," Dennis responded, "you sound just like my parents, nag, nag, nag. Let's get it straight—you want to screw up your life, that's up to you. I don't—so get off my back."

The subject changed. There was more laughing and rough-housing, more smell of burning underwear, but no more pressure to "take a hit." Dennis, whoever he was, had determined that he was not going to let drugs do to him what they had done to his brother. That inner conviction was bullet-proof.

Be forewarned: Teaching principles is more difficult than just setting rules. Principle-centered training requires open lines of communication. If those lines are broken in your home, your first task will be to repair them. Only then can you begin to teach the principles that change lives.

Teach Positive Thinking

I say something like "Teach positive thinking," and you might instantly respond, *I don't want any of that Norman Vincent Peale stuff.* Really, positive thinking is Bible stuff. It's encouraged throughout the book, and it's beautifully summarized in Philippians 4:8: "Finally, brothers, whatever is true, whatever is noble, whatever is right, whatever is pure, whatever is lovely, whatever is admirable—if anything is excellent or praiseworthy—think about such things."

Recently I was the guest speaker at a youth camp in Florida. It was a beautiful, well-appointed camp with many comforts. The cabins even had their own bathrooms. What a difference from the camp I attended as a kid, where if you saw "George Washington slept here" carved above the bunk, you could actually believe it. The Florida camp had a wonderful lake with canoes and tons of waterfront equipment. It had a basketball court, a volleyball court, a miniature racing track—all the things you dreamed of when you were a kid. As I stood admiring the facilities, two teenage girls walked by. "Hello," I said, "how's it going?"

The girl's one-word reply caught me completely off guard. "Bor-r-ring," she whined.

Was she serious? "But there's so much stuff here," I said. "What more would you need to make it exciting?"

She didn't even hesitate. "If there was a mall and television, I guess it would be okay."

A mall and television? What a shame that so many kids have lost their positive outlook and zest for life, their adventure options limited to television and shopping.

Today's typical high-school graduate has logged at least 15,000 hours before the small screen—more time than he has spent on any other activity except sleep. At present levels of advertising and mayhem, he will have been exposed to 350,000 commercials and vicariously participated in 18,000 killings.[1]

It's a problem, of course, that most of what our kids watch on TV teaches values directly opposite to those we hope they will develop. It's perhaps an even greater problem that those hours spent vegetating in front of the tube are hours during which there is no creativity being exercised, no personal interaction, no love being communicated. One of the best things you can do to help your kids develop positive thinking is

to move the television from its prominent place in your home to an upstairs room. Then open the window and throw it out.

A Louis Harris and Associates poll indicates that "Teenagers rank television as the fourth most important source of their information on both sex and birth control. . . . Their reliance on television is of concern because the survey shows that many teenagers . . . believe that TV gives a realistic picture of such topics as sexually transmitted diseases (45%), pregnancy (28%), and people making love (24%)."[2]

How tragic: Kids actually believe that the life they see depicted on TV is accurate! Watch five movies and five hours of television and tell me whether they were true-to-life and whether they were a positive influence. Do you come away from those hours of viewing feeling creative, worthwhile, enriched, and interested in life? Or do you come away feeling alienated and discouraged after viewing an excessive amount of mayhem, greed, murder, self-indulgence, blatant sensuality—and that's just the commercials! Unless a mutated turtle is beating the yogurt out of a radioactive alligator, or a drug pusher is ventilating someone with a sawed-off shotgun, or special effects are creating images bigger than life, today's kid is bored.

Don't let Hollywood shape your kid's view of the world.

We've allowed society to reverse the equation. Real excitement comes from *life*—not from illusions of life. Joy comes from participating, not from observing. Fulfillment comes from giving, not from buying. You and I have the opportunity and responsibility to demonstrate that kind of positive thinking for our kids. If we don't, they're not likely to see it anyplace else. If you allow your own life to be anaesthetized into routine by the tube, expect your kids to do the same.

It isn't just our dependence on the media that needs to change. We need to be more positive in *our* outlook on life.

You'd be amazed how your kids learn their outlook directly from you. I overheard parents teaching their children negative thinking at lunch one day. They had just come from church and were talking about people they'd seen there—and they didn't make a single positive comment about anyone. At one point in their criticism, the son interrupted to point out what he considered an ugly hairdo on the girl sitting across from them. "What a geek," the boy sneered. His mother added her own unkind remarks, then continued with her critique of yet another acquaintance. That son had undoubtedly learned his negative approach to life from his parents' example. It seemed likely to me that he would grow up to see only the negative in everybody and everything.

On another occasion, I was stuck in the Atlanta airport because of a flight cancellation. As the cancellation was announced, my immediate reaction was a flood of self-pity and anger—but it quickly disappeared when I heard a young mother who was to have been on the same flight say to her five-year-old daughter, "Just think—now we can eat a nice meal at the restaurant, and then we can play that space game you wanted to play." Good thing that five-year-old wasn't learning from the example of *my* attitude. Instead of teaching her child to allow circumstances to control her emotions, that young mother was teaching that an inner spirit of joy can be exercised even in difficult situations. She turned the inconvenience of a delayed schedule into opportunity. Instead of complaining about the stupid airlines, she used the time to build a relationship with her daughter.

Zig Ziglar says you have two options in reaction to life's trials: You get bitter or you get better. Demonstrating the skill of positive thinking can only help your kids get better.

Build on the Existing Foundation

In other words, don't try to make a rose out of tulip.

I never cease to be amazed at how different my two children are. From the moment of birth, they have demonstrated their own unique personalities. Traci was smiling when she was born. "Hi!" she said. "My name is Traci, and I love you." She cooed and cuddled and slept during normal hours. A dirty diaper was about the only thing that would make her cry.

After I'd lived with Traci for three years, Taryn announced her arrival. *Great,* I thought. *I already learned how to do the father thing with the first one—this will just be more of the same!* Was I wrong! Suddenly the rules changed. Taryn was a totally different person.

We knew that even before she was born. Back when Diane had been pregnant with Traci, when I would put my hand on Diane's stomach to feel the baby, Traci would gently push back in the very spot I was touching. Taryn, on the other hand, would kick and punch with every appendage available. You could see it. Once when I put my ear to Diane's tummy, I heard Taryn complaining about the food service.

When Taryn was born, she set out to prove that she wasn't like anyone else in the family. She screamed for the first six months of her life. She slept while we were awake and stayed awake while we tried to sleep. Taryn was *proud* of a dirty diaper; she would walk through the room with a little grin on her face, loaded diaper dragging on the ground. Taryn was what James Dobson calls a strong-willed child. She could have been the poster child for the Strong-Willed Kids Society. As it looks now, Traci will grow up to be a professional hairdresser (doing only her own hair). Taryn will be a missionary veterinarian terrorist. Each, obviously, is unique—and I have learned to love them for that uniqueness.

I remember being frightened just before Taryn was born. I loved Traci so much that I didn't know whether there would be any left over for anyone else. What a miracle! When she arrived, my love for her was just as intense as my love for Traci. God provided a reservoir of love that was sufficient for both. Yes, during those sleepless nights it would have been easy to decide that one personality was good and the other bad. And I must admit there were even moments when the words "frontal lobotomy" passed through my mind. But Taryn has grown to be her own person. I wouldn't change one thing about her. She's a fascinating creation of God who leaves a trail of laughter and insects wherever she goes. She reads several books a week, is conversant on just about any subject, and still exercises her strong will.

And I have learned that her strong-willed character trait is neither better nor worse than the more docile character of her sister. To try to change the foundational material God gave either of them would be a horrible mistake. Instead, I must build on those foundations and try to channel their behavior in positive directions. The same strong will that makes parenting Taryn a fascinating challenge keeps her from giving in to peer pressure. The social sensitivity that makes it so important for Traci to be with her friends is the same character that causes her friends to trust her for advice.

Ask yourself: "What are the unique qualities in each of my children?" Once you recognize those qualities, treat them like a precious seed. Nurture them and carefully direct the development of those gifts in positive directions.

**You build the character of a
strong-willed child not by destroying
his will, but rather by redirecting it.**

When I was a child, I loved to be in front of people. Some adults labeled me a show-off, hungry for attention, selfish, egotistical. And in some ways, they were right; the natural gifts that God had given me were often misdirected toward wrong behavior. But there was nothing wrong with those gifts. There is no doubt that God created in me a desire to perform. That desire is an integral part of who I am. An attack on that basic characteristic of my personality is an attack on me and an offense to my Creator. Those well-meaning folks who tried to change that characteristic instead of channeling my unique gifts in a positive direction were wrong. You build the character of a strong-willed child not by destroying his will, but rather by redirecting it. You build character in the life of a entertainer by building on the foundation that is already there.

One day my high-school English teacher invited me to stay after school. I knew this wasn't a social invitation because I had just spent the hour disrupting her class. She stared at me in silence for about a minute. (It reminded me of the silence that precedes a big tornado.) Then, quietly, she said, "Ken, I want you to go out for speech."

"Speech!" I sneered. "You've got to be kidding." All my friends walked around school wearing letter jackets with macho sports symbols on them—symbols like crossed hockey sticks, footballs, and baseball bats. I wasn't going to be caught walking around school with a set of lips hanging from my jacket. "What makes you think I can do anything in speech?" I asked.

She looked me right in the eye and said, "Ken, with a single sentence you can make everyone in this class laugh, destroying a teaching atmosphere it has taken me most of an hour to create. That takes ability. Why not use that ability in a positive way?"

She pestered me until I entered speech competition in the Humorous Interpretation category. I won almost every contest I entered. Because of her persistence and encouragement, today I travel full-time, using my gifts to entertain and help people. Most important, I use them to share around the world the wonderful message of God's love.

What enables me to do this? The same basic, God-given need to perform that drove people crazy and got me in lots of trouble as a kid. The foundation that a wise teacher chose to build on, rather than destroy. Build character on the unique foundation that God created in your child. Strengthen that foundation by encouraging creative and useful outlets for it.

You can, of course, try to destroy that unique foundation and build a new one more to your liking; many well-meaning parents do. But even if you're successful, which isn't likely, in the process you'll risk killing the self-esteem of your child. Better to teach them to make use of that foundation in ways that will please God and that will celebrate and exploit the way he designed your child.

Build Self-Esteem

I have been privileged over the years to speak to millions of teenagers across America. I've discovered in my informal conversations with thousands of them that the number-one problem faced by these dear kids is not drugs, promiscuity, or alcohol abuse. Those problems are symptoms of a deeper, more serious problem: lack of self-esteem.

Our teenagers can't see how valuable they really are. Every minute of the day, another teenager tries to end his or her life. The very act of attempting suicide is a denial of personal worth. I'm not going to try to place the blame for this tragic state of affairs, except to say that our society unknowingly promotes it. We assign great value to athletic ability, outward beauty, wealth, and intellect, forgetting that ninety-nine percent of our kids don't excel in those categories. We assign almost no value to the basic positive characteristics without which civilization would perish: love, compassion, charity, gentleness, kindness, humility.

So how do you and I combat society's misplaced values and rebuild self-esteem in our kids? The essential first step: recognizing the unique gifts and personality of our children. The necessary second step: recognizing and nurturing every positive inner value and conviction your child demonstrates. Far too often, we spend most of our time pulling weeds in the garden of our children's lives, instead of fertilizing the flowers. When our kids are "bad," we scold or correct them. When they are good, we say nothing. But the absence of rebuke does not register in a child's mind as a positive reinforcement. When your child shows compassion for another person, that compassion should be recognized and praised. Be on principle patrol every day. Sharing, good moral judgment, proper expression of anger, self-control—all these things should be observed and heaped with lavish praise. There are no Academy Awards or halls of fame for positive values or behavior; neither our educational systems nor society in general will present awards to honor your child for his upstanding principles. It's up to you to identify those positive characteristics and hand out the statues. Remember: It's not just the behavior you are praising—it's the values and convictions you see developing in your children.

For self-esteem to last, it must be built on a foundation that cannot be shaken. Here the Christian faith offers specific hope. Kids need to know that they are more than just a purposeless accident riding a planet to nowhere. I wish you could be with me to see the changes I've seen in the lives of kids who have come to believe that they were created with unique purpose and meaning. Joy replaces depression and excitement takes the place of apathy when kids learn that they were created in the image of God. Before God laid the foundations of the earth, he had your son's or daughter's picture on the wall. His design for their life is to make them uniquely like himself—like him in a way that no one else on the face of the earth can ever be. A rare stamp sells for thousands; a one-of-a-kind painting sells for millions. A one-of-a-kind person is priceless. And yet kids often get depressed because they're different! From birth, we need to tell them that their uniqueness is part of their immense value.

Far too often, we spend most of our time pulling weeds in the garden of our children's lives, instead of fertilizing the flowers.

An understanding of God's love helps builds self-esteem. His love for your kids (and for you) was demonstrated in the death of his *own* son. I wrote that sentence not to sound preachy or to make this book acceptable reading for a Christian audience—I wrote it because it is a truth that transforms lives and creates self-worth where before there was none. When I get up in the morning, it is not my international travel, my popularity as a speaker, or my recognition as an author that brings excitement and meaning to my life. Although I enjoy the benefits of all of those things, it is the realization that God loved me enough to give his son for *me* that fills my soul with fire and gives my life meaning, worth, and purpose.

One of the reasons I continue to share this message all over the world is that it brings hope to the hopeless of all ages. It brings self-worth and direction to lives that were once self-destructive, hostile, and aimless. If you want to build character in the life of your child, start by building self-esteem on an unshakable foundation of faith. Implant in your child's soul these truths:

You are priceless because you are unique.
You are priceless because God loves you just as you are.
You are priceless because of what Jesus paid to redeem you.
You are priceless because I love you just the way you are.

Have High Expectations

Bill Glass tells of bringing a pro football player to share his testimony with a group of men in prison. The football player explained that his father had always believed in him and had expected the best. He described the joy his accomplishments had brought to his father. "I lived up to my father's expectations," he said with pride.

An inmate quietly spoke up: "I, too, lived up to my father's expectations," he murmured.

Our own expectations will have dramatic effects on the lives of our kids. Motivational speaker Zig Ziglar says that we need to look for the gold in our kids. A gold miner is successful because he is willing to discard tons of dirt in the search for a small vein of gold. When he finds that gold, he carefully mines and refines it—and gains a fortune. Have high expectations. Look for the gold in your kids.

Cipher in the Snow is one of the most poignant films I have ever seen. Based on a true story, this film details the unexplainable death of a young boy. One day he stepped off the school bus and collapsed dead in the snow. During the investigation of his death, they discovered that no one could remember him. In the minds of everyone who knew him, he was a cipher, a zero. Some of his teachers couldn't even remember him being in their classes; at home, he was ignored and treated as though he had no worth. Since there was no other apparent cause of death, the most likely explanation was that he finally came to believe he was zero. Just like the convict, he lived up to expectations—he died quietly in a snowbank. He became zero.

There is a mountain of evidence that high expectations have the same effect—but in the opposite direction. I once asked a counselor how much I should expect from my children. He responded by saying, "Expect the best from your kids—then rejoice with whatever you get!"

The gold miner expects the best. He's hoping for a motherlode that will make him wealthy forever. But at the discovery of the smallest nugget, he dances and shouts for joy, momentarily suspending work in order to celebrate his wonderful discovery. He shows all his friends the precious nugget he has found. Then he returns to work, looking for more nuggets, still expecting the very best.

**Expect the best from your kids—then
rejoice with whatever you get.**

How often, when we talk with or about our children, do we concentrate on all the dirt we've excavated and on the tremendous amount of work we've put in without finding the motherlode. We don't see the nuggets because we're too busy concentrating on the dirt. It's time to start mining the gold in our children. Take that counselor's advice: Expect the best, and then rejoice over whatever you get. Slowly but surely, your children will live up—or down—to your expectations.

Teach Compassion

I believe in kids. I believe that they're capable of much more than we give them credit for. Yet many of us allow our children to go through life without ever tapping their potential for compassion. We allow them to grow up with a chronic case of ingrown eyeballs. They live self-centered lives, blind to the beauty and purpose of serving others. These are the kids who, as teens, consider going to the mall or owning their own car to be the ultimate experience.

But what a change comes over these same teens when they realize their potential to serve others! Every year, groups like

World Servants, Teen Missions International, and the Center for Student Missions take kids to third-world countries or poverty-stricken areas in the United States where those kids live in difficult, often uncomfortable circumstances to help people who are less fortunate than themselves. Every year, many of those kids come back changed forever. No longer do they feel that the world revolves around them and their desires. Their eyes have been opened to a great truth: Value in life comes not from getting as much as you can, but rather from giving.

Build compassionate children instead of conspicuous consumers.

The change brought about by this experience is most dramatic in the lives of teenagers who have all their lives been given everything. These children are also the ones who are most resistant to change. Nothing will inhibit character growth like never having to see or face any hardship.

Give your kids opportunities to serve. Let their hearts grow tender through the experience and privilege of reaching out to others.

Let Them Experience Pain

I love my girls so much that I want to come to their defense at every turn. But I also love them so much that I guard against that parental urge. While I want them to know that I'm available when they really need me, I also let them fight many of their own battles and face the negative consequences of their own actions—things they must learn to do if they're to survive.

I overheard a teenage girl talking to her father on a pay phone at a church camp. "Dad, please come and get us!" she complained. "The food is terrible, there are no phones in our room—and we're staying in *cabins!* Can you believe it, Dad?

Old-fashioned cabins with only one bathroom for four girls! Please come and get us."

That father didn't come to get them. Instead, he Federal-Expressed airline tickets for his daughter and two of her friends, and they left the next day.

My heart broke for those girls. If they ever do have to face adversity on their own, they're dead meat! And if they remain protected for the rest of their lives, the mediocrity and boredom will kill them. Those dear girls missed the excitement and fun of camp, the possibilities of relationships, the glory of spiritual renewal—all because it was a little inconvenient. They had been protected from every storm. The first bad winter, they'll be found beside the road.

Kids should also experience the consequences of their mistakes and misbehavior. Unfortunately, they often know how to avoid this by clever manipulation. "I promise I'll never do it again," they plead. "Please give me one more chance." But the sorrow in their voice is not remorse over having broken curfew by one hour and thereby disappointing and hurting their parents—it's remorse over having to face the consequence of being grounded this coming weekend. "If it were any other weekend, I wouldn't mind, Dad, but we've made special plans for this weekend."

It takes every bit of my will power not to give in to this. The tears and sorrow over a lost weekend are real. But if I give in, I insulate my child from the consequences of her behavior and set her up for deeper sorrow later in life. If every time a child forgets an assignment or lunch money you jump into the car and bring it to him, he'll never learn responsibility. When that child gets a job and forgets the keys to open the store, you won't be there to come to the rescue, and very likely the boss won't come to the rescue either.

Your child's ability to handle such responsibilities in adult life comes from what he is learning about taking responsibility now. I recently talked to a teacher who had seen a boy slap another boy smaller than himself. The teacher made the bully apologize in front of the class and stay after school. The bully's father threatened to sue unless the teacher retracted her accusation and publicly apologized to him. Unsupported by the school's administration, she capitulated in order to keep her job. If that is typical of this father's behavior, he is slowly signing the death warrant of his son. Someday, that boy will behave irresponsibly in a situation where his father won't be able to save him from paying the consequences.

Be fair with your children, be flexible, but above all, be consistent. Following through on consequences for misbehavior is sometimes heartbreakingly difficult, but from those unpleasant experiences grow roots of character that will make your child a survivor.

Teach Them to Wait

Another root of character your kids need to survive is the ability to wait.

As adults, we view time from a totally different perspective than our children. Time is compressed for adults; the years fly by. It seems like only yesterday I held my daughter in my arms as she snuggled close to my neck, fast asleep. Today she gives me tentative hugs and patronizingly pats me on the back. Yesterday she wouldn't leave the room without me. Today she's off with her friends at every opportunity and prefers that I don't go along. Sixteen years have passed since her baby years, but it seems like a heartbeat. Over the span of forty or fifty years of life, a year is just a blink. But at age four, a year is a quarter of a lifetime, and at sixteen, a year is "like totally forever."

Yes, it's hard for kids to wait—but the most effective men and women in ministry, in business, or in building loving families are those who have learned two important lessons: First, they have learned to set long-range goals; second, they have learned to wait patiently as they work daily toward those goals. For an adult, a long-range goal may be five or ten years in the future. Most teenagers can't even imagine five years; they figure they'll be in heaven by that time.

A smaller child might find it possible to work at a task for several minutes in order to achieve a goal, but probably not longer. The average teenager might be able to concentrate his or her efforts for a week, or even for a month if the goal is attractive enough. In a society that thrives on instant gratification, we need to encourage our children to look ahead and to be willing to wait. We should help them consider what they want to accomplish with their lives; we should encourage them to work each day to reach the goals of tomorrow. Unfortunately, there are many adults who never learned these tasks themselves; they'll have a hard time teaching them to their children.

A whole generation of young adults is living under impossible debt, helpless to control their own lives or experience financial freedom—all because they never learned to wait. In *I Don't Remember Dropping the Skunk, but I Do Remember Trying to Breathe* (Grand Rapids: Zondervan Publishing House, 1990), the survival manual I wrote for teenagers, I encouraged kids to put off purchases in order to learn this important discipline. "How many times have you bought something you thought you wanted only to discover that you never use it? Next time you're tempted to buy on impulse, write the item down on a piece of paper and wait thirty days," I counseled. Usually, at the end of thirty days, kids discover that they don't really need the item anymore. Now they want something else—and if this new desire goes onto the list for thirty days, it too will probably be unseated a month later by yet another item. Does that mean kids will never buy anything? No. It means that those items kids still decide to buy thirty days later are usually items they genuinely need or at least want badly enough to enjoy for a significant period of time.

Waiting is a wonderful clarifier of truth. Slavery to immediate gratification is the basis of many of the destructive experiences of adolescence and early adulthood, such as experimentation with drugs, premarital sex, and the bondage of debt. Teach kids to wait—help them say no to immediate gratification.

Teach Them to Love Doing Right

The inner satisfaction that comes from doing the right thing is another root of strength and character you can encourage in your kids. How do you encourage it? By praising and encouraging good behavior over and over again. Consistently expressing your pleasure over excellence teaches your children to find gratification in excellence. The reward of knowing that they have done their best can be reward enough.

This kind of determination in kids shows itself only in glimpses, and when it does, it must be nurtured and fed with much praise in order to grow. Like the prospector looking for gold, watch for this root of character growing in your children. Don't get so caught up in dealing with everyday crises that you miss the nuggets among the tailings. Challenge yourself to be as creative in parenting as you are in other facets of your life. Keep an eye out for teachable moments that may be remembered forever.

It is not what a person dreams that
determines what he will become.
It is what a person does
every day of his life.

I was almost flunking out of Oak Hills Bible College when a professor called me into his office. After a brief period of small talk, he leaned across the desk and asked a question that no one had ever asked me before: "What do you dream of becoming?"

I had to think a bit, but I finally responded with an outline of the lofty goals I had set for my life.

"Why, then," he asked, "when you have such lofty goals, do you live with this kind of mediocrity?" My face reddened as he slid my midterm grades across the desk. I could only stammer as I searched for an excuse. Then, in that teachable moment, he said something I have never forgotten. "You say you aspire to excellence, yet you settle for mediocrity." He tapped those horrible grades with his finger. "Ken, it is not what a person dreams that determines what he will become. It is what a person does every day of his life." Then came the necessary encouragement: "I believe you are capable of all you have dreamed, Ken. Why don't you start living as though *you* believe it?"

I graduated near the top of my class.

Now let me encourage you in the same way. I believe that you are capable of living the kind of life that will help build the roots of strength and character in your kids. *But it isn't enough to just dream about it*. How you respond to your kids today is what makes you the parent you are. Start today to mine the gold and nourish the roots that will sustain your kids tomorrow.

8

The Talk

*Everything You Want Your Kids to Know
About Sex But Are Too Chicken
to Tell Them*

SEX!

There it is, in capital letters, right in front of your eyes. What a nasty word to associate with your baby—and yet during your child's early adolescent years, scads of hormones are turned loose in his or her body dedicated to awakening this drive, whether you like it or not. One evening your little boy goes to bed dreaming of wild horses and ice cream, and the next morning he wakes up with hair all over his body and an undeniable interest in the opposite sex. Your little girl wakes up one morning fascinated with boys, when yesterday they were nothing but nasty little pests. If you think this is confusing for you as a parent, try to remember how confused a kid feels during this time.

There are few times when courageous parenting is more needed. There is a tremendous outcry today because the school systems are teaching sex education devoid of moral guidelines. In some schools, condoms are passed out by health officials like aspirins were in our day. We *should* cry out—but not until we realize that some of the blame for this dangerous state of affairs can be placed at our own doorstep. The true responsibility for sex education is ours, parents. And more often than not we drop the ball. I was amazed, while speaking to a group of teenagers recently, to discover that over half claimed they had never had a significant talk with their parents about sex. In a poll published in *People* magazine, 31 percent of teenagers say their parents rarely talk about sex, and 22 percent say their parents *never* talk with them about sex.[1]

A father in Texas told me that he had bought a book on the subject, tossed it into his son's room with the command, "Read this," and was halfway to work before it hit the floor. He was glad the job was over. A mom in Iowa mentioned nervously to her daughter that she wanted to discuss the subject. That's as far as she got; her daughter rolled her eyes in disgust and embarrassment, and the mom retreated in fear. Most parents avoid the discussion altogether or hope that somehow their kids will be able to read between the lines of "Be good" or "Be careful."

That's just not enough. Because of the misinformation they're getting on this vital subject, our kids are destroying themselves. We need to step out of the passive role we've adopted and move toward being a positive influence in the sex education of our children. I hope these suggestions will help.

Know What You're Talking About

A small boy, ready to begin preparing a report for school, first made his way to the kitchen to talk to his mother. "Mom," he asked, "Where did I come from?"

The boy's mother had been meaning to talk with him about this important subject, but she wasn't really ready and she was very busy at the moment, so she put him off with the old saw, "The stork brought you."

On the way back to his room, the boy saw his grandmother sitting in her chair, quietly knitting. "Grandma," he asked, "Where did I come from?"

Grandma wasn't about to open that can of worms, so she said, "The stork brought you, just as he brought your mother and me."

With that, the little boy went back to his room, picked up his pencil, and began his report with these words: "There hasn't been a normal birth in our family for three generations!"

It is important that *you* know the truth about sex; otherwise, your kids will conclude that you're still living in the age of Fred Flintstone and Barney Rubble. It isn't enough to be satisfied with the information you had when you were a kid. The world has changed dramatically. The kids in your community, in your child's school, and yes, even in your church, are more sexually active than you think.

"From 1971 to 1985 teen sexual activity rates have risen 67 percent," reports the Family Research Council.[2] And according to a Planned Parenthood poll:

> Almost three out of every ten teenagers (28%) aged 12–17 say they have had sexual intercourse. The proportion increases with age. From 4% of the 12-year-olds and 10% of the 13-year-olds up to 46% of the 16-year-olds and 57% of the 17-year-olds. Thus more than half of all teenagers report they have had sex by their seventeenth year.[3]

When I hear information like this about teenagers and sex in America, I'm frightened. I want to bury my head in the sand and say it isn't true—or that it might be true for some degenerate segment of our society, but certainly not my town or my kids' school. And *certainly* not our church. Yet our kids, even without reading the results of a survey, know what's going on. They live every day in the world from which these cold statistics are generated. If you attempt to talk to them about sexuality without knowing something about the world they live in, your words will carry little weight.

Promiscuous sex can kill.

There's another important reason for educating yourself: the safety of your child. When I was in high school, the greatest danger of promiscuous behavior was the possibility of pregnancy. In college, I became aware of the epidemic of syphilis as it spread across the nation. In the late seventies and early eighties, the dreaded result of uncontrolled passion was herpes. But all of those were, to some extent, curable or at least preventable. Today's message is more urgent. Promiscuous sex can kill. AIDS has changed everything. AIDS is spreading across our country like wildfire, affecting not just prostitutes and homosexuals and drug addicts but also sexually active heterosexual teens who thought they were safe. At the end of 1989, the number of AIDS cases in American teenagers had increased by 40 percent over the last two years. There is still no cure for AIDS. Despite the fact that some misguided individuals are teaching the message of "safe sex," abstinence is still the only effective protection from this dreaded killer.

Accept the Responsibility

Sex education should not be left in the hands of the schools or friends or television. Not only do these sources distort the purpose of God's beautiful creation, they also unwittingly disseminate some very dangerous information about it. While schools are allowing assemblies that promote safe sex (meaning the use of condoms), you should know—and so should your kids—that the evidence proves condoms are *not* effective in preventing AIDS.

At the International Conference on AIDS in Washington, D.C., June 1–5, 1987, research was presented revealing that, among couples with one HIV positive and one HIV negative partner, after an eighteen-month period, the number of negative partners who tested positive after practicing abstinence for that entire period was zero. Among those who used a condom during that period, *seventeen percent* tested positive. Using a condom for "safe sex" has almost the identical odds of Russian roulette.

Even the so-called sex experts no longer talk about condoms and safe sex in the same breath. Their own studies show that it just isn't true. Yet, in thousands of schools, kids are still encouraged to use condoms as a means of safe sex. Although the "safe sex" advocates have good intentions, they're simply not telling the truth. In "Ten AIDS Myths Answered," Dr.

Theresa L. Cremshaw says, "Condoms with an infected person are deadly."[4]

Much of the information kids get about sex comes from friends. This is like the blind leading the blind. Just a few days ago, I heard a girl who is a junior in high school explain that you can't get pregnant if you only "do it" (have sex) a few times. This poor girl is five months pregnant, and she *still* believes this lie. She wonders why she's the exception to the rule! In a discussion on sex, a senior boy argued that you can't get AIDS if you take a good soapy shower right after having sex. He had heard this from a friend, and he insisted that it was true even after he'd heard plenty of information that proved it false. Your kids will get tons of information about sex from their friends. Most of it is dangerously incorrect.

Using a condom for "safe sex" has almost the identical odds of Russian roulette.

Another major source of information on sex for your kids is the media, primarily television and the movies. I can't remember seeing either a television program or a movie in the last several years that responsibly handled this subject. The media treats sex like a sport. Morally responsible characters are laughed off the screen, and almost every relationship, no matter how casual, winds up in bed. Donald Wildmon of the National Foundation for Decency says that TV viewers see nine thousand sex scenes on the tube every year, fewer than 6 percent of them involving married people. The not-so-subtle message is extremely powerful: It's natural, everybody's doing it, get with the program. Even advertising capitalizes on this irresponsible approach to one of God's most beautiful creations with double-entendre slogans like *"Just Do It."*

And now I'm going to say the same thing about talking to your kids about sex: Just do it. If you're not willing to teach your kids about the beauties of sex within the guidelines of God's divine purpose—and about the dangers of stepping outside those guidelines—*no one else will.* Please make yourself aware of the truth and teach your kids how to use this wonderful gift of God.

I've written this chapter not to educate you about sex, but rather to motivate you to take an active role in letting your kids know the truth. I would like to recommend some very good books for your kids, but *you* should read them first. Then ask your kids to read them (or read them aloud to the younger kids) and *make it a point to discuss the material with them.* Don't, like that father in Texas, simply toss the book at them and run.

Who Made Me? by Malcolm and Meryl Doney. Humorously illustrated by Nick Butterworth and Mick Inkpen. Grand Rapids: Zondervan Publishing House, 1987. A read-aloud, facts-of-life book for younger children.

In the Beginning: Teaching Your Children About Sex—Ages 4 to 7 by Mary Ann Mayo. Illustrated. Grand Rapids: Zondervan Publishing House, 1991.

God's Good Gift: Teaching Your Children About Sex—Ages 8 to 11 by Mary Ann Mayo. Illustrated. Grand Rapids: Zondervan Publishing House, 1991.

Talking with Your Kids About Love, Sex & Dating by Barry and Carol St. Clair. San Bernardino: Here's Life Publishers, 1989.

Why Wait? What You Need to Know About the Teen Sexuality Crisis by Josh McDowell and Dick Day. San Bernardino: Here's Life Publishers.

Handling Your Hormones: The "Straight Story" on Love & Sexuality, Revised Edition by Jim Burns. Eugene, Oregon: Harvest House, 1986.

Next Time I Fall in Love: How to Handle Sex, Intimacy, and Feelings in Dating Relationships, by Chap Clark. Grand Rapids: Zondervan Publishing House, 1987.

Another terrific resource for increasing your own knowledge about sexuality, as well as for giving you some terrific photocopyable tools—quizzes, fact sheets, and so on—to pass out to your kids, is a book designed for youth workers: *Teaching the Truth About Sex: Biblical Sex Education for*

Today's Youth by David Lynn and Mike Yaconelli. Grand Rapids: Zondervan Publishing House, 1990.

Make Sex Education Continuing Education

Most families think of sex education as "The Talk." The anguish and embarrassment surrounding "The Talk" have provided lots of laughs in countless TV shows and movies. If you try to educate your kids about sex with one talk during their lifetime, then there's no way to avoid that embarrassment and anxiety. Nor is there any way to adequately convey to your kids what sex is really about. Sex education should be more than that.

In the book *Talking with Your Kids About Love, Sex & Dating,* Barry and Carol St. Clair include a chapter entitled, "The Talks"—not "The Talk." Plural. Barry says,

> Normally, "The Talk" doesn't move us toward our goal of effective communication with our children. Because of that, we need to think through how we can have on-going communication with our children about love, sex and dating.[5]

The insight that you can give your kids about sex and love will be more valuable to them than a truckload of diamonds. But if you wait until one sunny day in puberty to back up the truck and dump the whole load on your kid, you'll probably kill him. You'll certainly make both of you very uncomfortable. Healthy attitudes about sex should be built from the very first years of a child's life. Listen for leading questions; watch for teachable moments; use some of the books I've listed above for a variety of age groups.

Teach Your Kids That Sex Is Not Dirty or Evil

Unfortunately, there are some parents who unwittingly hold on to the old dualistic idea that the body is dirty and evil. This was one of the original heresies of the church many centuries ago. It's just as heretical today. Satan didn't slip into the creation lab and give humans sex organs while God was on a coffee break. We are created in the image of God—and that means that *all* our parts are honoring to him and are there

because he put them there. Refusing to discuss our sexuality implies that it is dirty.

Giving cute names to body parts does the same thing. In forty-five years of living, I have never heard ears referred to as waxy willies or eyes as looky-loos, yet the list of names that enable us to avoid saying *penis* or *vagina* would fill this page. At the end of a conference, a lovely grandmother came up to me. "Do you have any books on . . . [long pause] . . . you know . . . [another pause, looking around to make sure no one would hear] . . . sex?" she asked, in a hoarse whisper. "I want to get something like that for my grandson," she continued. "I've looked at some of the stuff Josh McDowell has written, but he's so *direct*. Do you have anything that beats around the bush more?" Those are her exact words. I was so taken aback by what she said that I asked her to excuse me and ran off to write it down.

The lies our society tells us about sex do not beat around the bush—they are direct and aggressive. We must be just as direct with the truth. From the very beginning, kids need to get answers to their questions about sex in a direct and honest fashion. The word *stork* should never appear in any answer to the question "Where did I come from?" The amount of detail you provide in that answer will depend on the age and maturity of the child. But be sure to include, from the very beginning, the information that kids are a wonderful gift from God, a gift given to mommies and daddies who express their love in a very special way.

If your child probes for more information with questions like "How did I get in your tummy?" don't reach for the stork or a head of cabbage. Those questions mean that it's time to continue your child's sex education with details of the beautiful and wonderful truth. While our girls were still very young, we sat down with them and read the book *Where Did I Come From?* This straightforward, honest portrayal of how babies come about is a wonderful tool for parents, with drawings included. I was amazed at Traci and Taryn's direct, detailed questions, as well as their lack of embarrassment. In a couple of places they laughed, and we laughed with them. But mostly they expressed a simple and innocent desire to know.

Because this book doesn't address God's part in creation, we took special pleasure in explaining his role in giving us this wonderful gift.

The lies society tells us about sex are direct and aggressive. We must be just as direct with the truth.

When their questions were all answered, the girls closed the book and went on to other play. But for several days, other questions would come to their minds, and they would ask them. There was no brooding, unhealthy curiosity or shock; as soon as they got honest answers to their honest questions, they were free to get on with being a kid.

In the years that followed, they sometimes expressed puzzlement over friends who snickered and whispered about sex. I explained that their friends had not had the privilege of hearing the truth; that was why they were sneaky and secretive and thought of sex as something naughty. And that, fellow parent, is precisely why we should always be reassuring our children with the truth. If you don't answer their questions honestly, they will get their answers from snickering friends and irresponsible television programming. Even worse, they may be attracted to pornography and fall under the spell of the greatest lie of all.

A warning is in order here. If you're successful in creating a comfortable atmosphere for your young children to discuss sex with you, they may also feel perfectly comfortable talking about sex with everybody else. That can create not only embarrassing situations but also hard feelings. It's wise to carefully explain to your kids that not everyone sees sex the way God intended and that some are offended or embarrassed by it. Even though our bodies are beautiful and special, we don't walk around naked; that's because we live in a sinful world. For the same reason, sex is a personal and special gift that is best discussed with the people you love.

A pastor friend told me that after he and his wife spent a

wonderful afternoon explaining the beauty of sex to their little daughter Sally, she was so excited she told all her friends. The parents of one of her friends reacted indignantly. Over the phone she asked how a pastor's daughter could have such a filthy mouth. No amount of explaining helped. This misguided woman insisted that her daughter would have no more contact with Sally. Encourage your younger children to ask their questions and express their views about sex at home—not because talk about sex is bad, but because many people just don't understand. Explain this to your children for their own sakes, as well as to avoid the embarrassment of others; the insensitive remarks of an offended adult who tells your child that he or she has a filthy mouth can undo all you've tried to teach.

Sally, my pastor friend's daughter, was not at all intimidated by the negative response of her friend's parents. That evening, as one of the elders of the church visited their home, she asked point-blank, "Mr. Smith, do you have a penis?"

Mr. Smith was wiser than the woman who had called earlier. He smiled and said, "That's a good question, Sally. Have your mom and dad been telling you about the wonderful way God brought you into the world?"

Sally's dad sat in uncomfortable silence as his little girl delivered a blow-by-blow, detailed account of all she had been taught. Then Sally's real question came to light: "Why don't you have any kids?" she asked.

Seeing a nod of consent from the pastor, Mr. Smith said, "Sally, I have all the parts that God gave your daddy and other men in the world. And I have loved my wife in the special way that brought you to your mom and dad. But babies are still a gift from God. Sometimes God allows babies to come from that love, and sometimes he doesn't. I hope you and your dad and mom will pray that God will bring my wife and me a baby from the love that we have for one another."

With her mind now free because her question had been answered without scorn or shame, Sally went off to play.

If only all of humanity could be responsible and sensitive enough to give children such an answer! I would rather see my girls take part in conversations such as that and go away confident of their sexuality than to have them learn the lies taught in a locker room, on a television show, or between the pages of a dehumanizing pornographic magazine. In teaching your kids discretion about where this subject is discussed, be careful not to slip back into the "sex is dirty" trap.

Teach the Joy of Sex

Teach the positive along with the negative. Too often our discussions with our kids about sex are restricted to the negative: premarital sex and its possible consequences. We also have a responsibility to tell our kids that God intended for us to enjoy sex within the bonds of marriage.

Have you ever read the Song of Solomon? If not, put this book down and read it before you continue. Finished? No, the Song of Solomon isn't another sneaky plot of Satan—it's part of the inspired Word of God. Obviously God is neither ashamed of nor prudish about sex, nor would he expect us to be. Those who oppose moral purity offer this argument: Why would God create us to enjoy sex and then restrict us from enjoying it? The truth is that the most powerful enjoyment of sex comes not from responding to every glandular stimulus, but rather by lifting sex to the place of honor it deserves: an unselfish (and unequaled) physical expression of love between married people. God does not restrict the use of sex to keep us from enjoying it. He restricts its use before marriage so that we might enjoy it to its fullest.

How can this concept be taught to our children? Probably through demonstration of a warm, loving relationship more effectively than through verbal communication. When children see moms and dads hugging and expressing love to one another, they glimpse (and, at some level, understand) far more than they actually see. I think that kids at those moments are subconsciously aware (even if they don't understand the mechanism by which it is done) of the secret moments when mom and dad fully express their love for each other. The intimacy contained in our open expressions of love with our spouse is nurtured by a private and very intimate sexual experience. If that's true in your marriage, there will come a time when you will be able to explain that to your kids verbally. If it's not true, then let's face it—it's going to be much more difficult to discuss with your kids the beauty of sex. And if infidelity and secret sexual sin permeate your life, then the job of educating your children about the joy of sex becomes almost impossible. One of the best ways to prepare for talking about sex with your kids is to strive for purity and commitment in your own life. Nurture the relationship you have with your spouse so that it can be exhibit A in your explanation of the joys of sex.

If the human spirit, even with the help of God, is incapable of resisting temptation, then indeed we are nothing more than animals.

Another value that needs to be taught from the beginning of a child's life and reinforced daily until our children leave our care is *self-control*. In an ABC television report on the spread of AIDS in our society, Connie Chung and fellow guests smirkingly dismissed abstinence before marriage as an archaic impossibility. Talk-show hosts Donahue and Geraldo have a parade of guests who talk as though only a demented fanatic would expect purity in this day and age. In fact, Phil Donahue states his view boldly in his book *The Human Animal*:

> Today girls reach puberty at about twelve years and boys at thirteen. Marriage is at least seven or eight years away and maybe ten or fifteen. Yet mom and dad and the local clergyman and everybody else says, "Wait." Wait for ten years? How can anyone wait for ten years when the radio is blasting out songs like, "I'm So Excited" and "What's Love Got to Do with It?"; when television is filled with steamy soap operas, "T and A," risque humor, and music videos; when movies lump virgins and nerds in the same category of undesirables; and finally, when that once in a lifetime rush of hormones is lighting fires in all the wrong places?[6]

In the *Rocky Mountain News,* Wednesday, August 28, 1991, a prominent minister proclaimed, "Counseling abstention is like taking a kid into a candy store and telling him he can't eat anything. It's not realistic."[7]

What a hopeless lot we are as a human race if we are slaves to our glands! If the human spirit, even with the help of God, is incapable of resisting temptation, then indeed we are nothing more than animals. Those who reject the validity or possibility of abstinence do disservice to the dignity of the human spirit as well as to the power of God. Perhaps this truth was most eloquently communicated in a column by Ann Landers. A young man wrote:

> Dear Ann,
>   I have been sleeping with three women for several months. Until a few days ago, none of them knew that the others existed and things were going fine. By chance, two of them met each other, compared notes, and found me out. Now they are furious with me. What am I going to do?
>   P.S. Please don't give me any of your moral junk.
>   Signed, Trapped.

Ann Landers answered like this:

> Dear Trapped,
>   The one major thing that separates the human race from animals is a God-given sense of morality. Since you don't have a sense of morality, I strongly suggest you consult a veterinarian.[8]

Our kids need to know that the discipline and self-control possible in our lives because of God's grace set the human race apart from the animal kingdom. We are not merely human animals, as Phil Donahue's book suggests. We are children of God.

Our children need to be taught to be proud of, rather than ashamed of, the moral values and disciplines they set in their lives. Just as self-respect and excellence are the products of a disciplined life, happy marriages and healthy, joyful sex are the products of a disciplined sex life. God created humankind in his own image and gave us the wonderful gift of sexual expression. He also gave us some guidelines to enjoy that expression to its fullest. Teach your children to be proud that they are operating according to the Owner's Manual. Teach them to look forward to the rewards of "doing it right"; demonstrate in your own life the benefits of purity.

In her notorious bestseller *Fear of Flying*, Erica Jong tried to give us a glimpse of what sex has to offer. Her book was a misguided effort. In the bestseller of all time, *The Holy Bible*, God has given us a much better guide to joyful sex. Pass those principles on to your children.

9
Dancing With the Wolves

Dealing With the Issues That Hound All Parents

A s I interviewed parents in preparation for writing this book, our conversations often focused on a few common issues. In discussion groups, enthusiasm would sometimes lag until one of these issues was brought up—then you couldn't get people to stop talking. This chapter takes a closer look at three of those issues—common problems that hound most parents. Not every family struggles with these problems to the same degree, but somewhere in this chapter you'll probably find a wolf that's barking up the right tree. What you won't find are surefire solutions. But these suggestions should at least take you a step in the right direction.

And if nothing else, you can take comfort in the fact that you're not alone. Nearly every family fights these same wolves.

100 Square Feet of National Disaster

Nothing is more disconcerting to a parent than to raise children in a clean, tidy environment only to have them choose to keep their own rooms like a pigsty. Occasionally I run into parents who tell me that their children keep their rooms immaculate without being asked, but I must confess that I never saw any of those rooms. When I looked skeptical after one mother made that claim, she offered to prove her point by inviting us over to see her son's neat room. She called back a few minutes later to ask if we could wait an hour so that she could pick up a few loose ends. I have a sneaky feeling she opened the door to that room and found wall-to-wall loose ends.

How do you get kids to clean up their room? Here are some options.

1. Coercion. Negative coercion consists of threatening a millennium of grounding or the loss of a special privilege (like breathing) until the room is spotless. Unfortunately, it's a short-term solution and requires more time and energy to enforce than most parents have. Even when it's successful, the room will stay clean only long enough to duck the consequences; then the loose ends take over again.

Even positive reinforcement won't guarantee a spotless room. We actually saw the carpet in Taryn's room for about a week as she anticipated the new room she would move into when we built an addition. Only if she kept her original room clean, you see, could she move into the new room. And when the transfer was complete, she worked hard at keeping her new room clean for about three days, then once again her room looked like the pictures I have seen of post-war Europe. Coercion is ineffective and does not have long-lasting results.

2. Force. I once told Taryn she would have to stay in her room until it was clean. It took seven tearful hours for her to accomplish what should have been a fifteen-minute task. She would begin cleaning, and then run across an interesting book or a bundle of pictures. When I checked up, I would find her sitting on the floor, happily reading or playing with a long-lost toy. Like coercion, force works for the moment, but it doesn't instill in your children a sense of pride in keeping their own room clean. I have decided that the use of force to induce a child to keep his or her room clean is cruel and unusual punishment. Force causes more conflict than it's worth.

3. The scientific approach. A wiser course, in my opinion, is a loving enforcement of the second law of thermodynamics coupled with deliberate temporary blindness. The second law of thermodynamics, in layman's terms (the only terms I understand), states that the universe is slowly disintegrating and running out of energy. We humans have become part of this process as we steadily mess up our planet to the point that our ability to live here is threatened. The same law applies to kids' rooms. Sooner or later, if a parent doesn't step in first, kids will need a piece of clothing that has languished in mildew long enough to take on a hue of green that makes it unwearable. Your careful explanation that you will be happy to wash the offensive item on your regular washing schedule when it finds its way to the hamper will be met with howls of protest: "But I need it right now!" Put the ball where it belongs—back in your child's court. Let her know that if she treats her clothes properly, they'll be available when needed, but that you have no intention of interfering with natural law by doing a special washing. It's her decision whether to have clean clothes available or not. In this way, your children learn the natural consequences of slovenly housekeeping.

It's perfectly all right to offer help—to, for instance, place a receptacle for dirty clothing in your child's room (the bigger the better). This kind of help encourages responsibility rather than rewarding irresponsibility.

For some reason, cleaning a badly littered room seems like an insurmountable task to a child. Don't expect perfection. Your view of a clean room and your kid's view are miles apart. I have come, after long struggle, to accept the pile of stuffed animals in the corner as a compromise; my adult preference, of course, would be to see them carefully stored in neat rows.

When things get out of control and your son needs a compass to find his bed, encourage him by agreeing to help. This doesn't mean that *you* clean the room. It means that you help him get started, then help him lay out the job in several bite-size, manageable tasks so that he can see it isn't going to take him the rest of his life. I no longer insist that the girls stay in their room until it's clean—primarily because I'm over forty and not sure I would live that long. Now, I set a time limit and reward the finished work with tons of praise and some special privilege or activity. Sometimes I will require only a portion of the task to be done each day.

Okay, I'll be honest. Occasionally I backslide and threaten that they'll never leave the house again until the room is clean.

When you've made it clear that your child has to suffer the natural consequences of a dirty room, the next step—and the hardest one, for many of us—is to develop temporary blindness. Close the door to the mess and don't look. You'll live longer, you'll fight with your kids less, and you won't be upset all the time. Dr. James Dobson says that we have to choose our battles carefully. Family life is too full of real concerns and conflicts to spend time battling over things that don't matter. Millions of kids have grown up in rooms that would have troubled a mother pig. Can you think of anyone who has failed in life because of it? Some of those adolescent pigs have even grown up to become presidents and millionaires. Contrary to our gut reactions, no person has ever become a bag lady because of a dirty room.

Why am I confident in the advice I have given? It's certainly not because my kids have spotless rooms. Rather, it's because they are improving. It's because we don't constantly fight over this issue like we used to. And it's because, as I write this, I am looking at a hotel room that would cause my own mother to faint. But I didn't turn out to be such a bad guy.

The Sunday Mornin' Blues

I'll never forget the shiver of fear that ran down my spine the first time I heard the words, "I don't want to go to church!" *She's only four years old*, I thought, *and already she's moving toward atheism*. Of course that wasn't the case at all. She just didn't want to go to church. Almost all children say those words at some point in their lives. How should a parent respond? Certainly not in panic; seldom is this a desire to abandon the faith. Try these steps instead:

1. **Ask the right questions.** Rather than reacting with outrage or disappointment, find out why your child doesn't want to go. A mom from Louisiana told me that she was devastated when her seven-year-old son, Carson, announced that he wasn't going to church anymore. After a long, impassioned lecture about the importance of going to church,

she finally paused long enough to ask Carson why he didn't want to go. "Because it's stupid," he responded.

Holding back her anger at this disrespectful if not slightly blasphemous outburst, she asked, "Why do you think it's stupid?"

His answer astounded her. "Because of the handkerchiefs," he said. Which leads to the next step:

2. Know what your child is being taught, and how. That Louisiana mother asked Carson to explain about the handkerchiefs, and she listened to his answer. Every Sunday, he said, the teacher would check to see which children were "good citizens." Fingernails and ears were inspected to see whether they were clean, the children were asked whether they had brushed their teeth, and each one had to show that he had a clean handkerchief. Carson didn't own a handkerchief, and he was embarrassed to ask his parents to get him one. Every Sunday, the kids who passed inspection would receive little stars they could paste on a paper crown—their reward for being good citizens. Carson's crown was empty.

And Carson was right—this *was* stupid.

Regardless of the good intentions of the teacher, every Sunday he was facing unnecessary embarrassment. Carson's wise mom presented him with a bright white handkerchief with his initials in the corner and the reassurance that he was a good citizen whether he carried it or not. She then tactfully helped the teacher understand the emotional consequences of this little exercise. Carson no longer wants to skip church. Which leads to the third step:

3. Work with your church to make sure that your child's learning experience is enjoyable. A church that is meeting your needs may be falling far short in meeting the spiritual needs of your children. An adult wouldn't continue going to a church that was dry and boring, but many parents insist that their children attend classes that are just that. The methods that keep the attention of a preschooler don't work for first graders. Junior-high boys and girls will probably begin begging to stay home if they're lumped in with the little kids. Asking kids of any age to sit still during a boring sermon is asking more than their little bodies can absorb. Even so, I've seen very small children receive spankings or severe scoldings because they couldn't sit still.

A better idea than spankings: Why not make your church aware of the needs expressed by your children? Then offer to help implement changes.

One of the most important things you can do for the spiritual health of your child is to establish, early in his life, a positive image of worship. Kids aren't content-oriented; they're experience-oriented. No matter how good the content, no matter how true it is to Scripture, if the lesson is given in unpleasant and unimaginative ways or if the truth is connected with embarrassing experiences (as it was with Carson and his handkerchiefs), your child will want to stay away.

4. Help your kids enjoy church. By discussing the things they're learning and by asking them to teach you what they have learned, you can help your children enjoy church. Show an intense interest in what they do in class. Young children especially enjoy playing the role of teacher. Take time after church to have them teach you what they have learned. Your interest can help make them excited about going to church. During the week, emphasize the lesson by challenging each other to practically apply the truth that was taught. If you make it fun, you may find that your children begin looking forward to church.

5. Give your kids alternatives. The advice given in the preceding paragraph—"Make it fun"—is much easier to implement with small children. Teenagers are another matter. Their desire to sleep in on Sunday is often part of their struggle for independence. Even so, their loss of interest can often be remedied by the right church youth program. Your church doesn't have to feature top musical artists or have extravagant social programs to gain the interest of a teenager. What it does need is an atmosphere of loving acceptance, a commitment to biblical truth, and a program that presents that truth in interesting (and by that I mean interesting to a teenager) and applicable ways. And besides that, there needs to be enough kids to make it a group. Teenagers are the most socially oriented creatures on the face of the earth. A church that offers teenagers a loving community of kids their own age who are working together to learn more about the Lord will attract many more.

It's possible to force reluctant teenagers to go to church, but if we've given them such a negative reaction to church attendance that they refuse to attend as adults, we've done more harm than good. Because the impression our teenagers gain of church is so important, we should be willing to go out of our way to give them the opportunity to worship and fellowship where they are taught sound biblical doctrine in an atmosphere of loving community. If your church isn't offering that opportunity to your teenagers, there are a few ways you can hope to provide it. You can take an active role in the development of a good youth program at your church. You can find a youth program in another church to supplement the worship opportunities your teenager finds at your own church. Or you can change churches.

Change churches? Isn't that a little drastic?

Yes. But sometimes it's necessary. When Traci turned twelve, she began to lose interest in church. Until then, she had seemed to enjoy Sunday school and had actually looked forward to going each Sunday. It didn't take us long to discover the reason for her loss of interest: In the entire church, there were only two kids her age. For many years, Diane and I had enjoyed the excellent Bible teaching and small, friendly atmosphere of that church. But because I wanted our daughters to have a positive worship experience through their teen years, we searched for a church with a good youth program and switched. I have never regretted that decision. The youth program in our present church is far from perfect. (There are no perfect programs.) But our daughters enjoy it, look forward to each meeting, and learn basic Christian beliefs and values. They also participate actively in the regular worship service. They must be getting what they need, because I see both of them growing spiritually and socially.

Insisting that your children attend church ("Why? Because I said so, that's why!") teaches them merely that you want them to go to church. Working with your children to discover what their needs are, and working with the church to enrich their worship experience, teaches them that you place a high value on their spiritual growth. There's a difference. Your willingness to make sacrifices to ensure that they are in an environment where they can grow will not go unnoticed.

Sibling Rivalry

Dinnertime at the Davis home. The meal is quiet, pleasant—until suddenly:

"Mom, she's looking at me."

"I'm not looking at you, ya little creep."

"Yes you are. I saw you."

"If you saw me, then you must have been looking at me first."

"Why would I look at something as ugly as you?"

A growl rumbles in my throat as I carefully put down a forkful of food and, with a meaningful look around the table, pick up a steak knife. "If I hear any more of that, you can both go to your room without eating," I say, teeth clenched.

"But she started it," they both protest in unison.

Plates rattle as my hand slaps the table. "That's it! If you can't talk pleasantly, then you'll go hungry!" I learned that approach from a book on how to deal with sibling rivalry. The book said that hunger should solve the problem. Fat chance. As they bump down the hallway on the way to their rooms, I hear this muted exchange:

"Now look what you've done! Just because I looked at you."

"That's okay. I'd rather starve than have you look at me."

"Creep."

"Double creep."

How can two people with family blood flowing in their veins fight so viciously and constantly and still claim that they love each other? What can a parent do to make it stop?

Our car is another battleground. Sometimes I wonder if we shouldn't install ropes and a bell to keep track of the rounds. It doesn't do any good to lose my temper and yell. Even reaching back to grab the kids doesn't work—long ago, they calculated the exact length of my arm, and they're experts at staying just out of reach. My wife, Diane, has an amazing ability: She can leave the driver's seat going sixty-five miles an hour, crawl into the back to administer justice, and return to the driver's seat without leaving the road. Yet no sooner is she back in the driver's seat than the battles begin again. In their wonderful book *Parenting with Love and Logic*, Foster Cline and Jim Fay suggest stopping the car and making the kids get out and walk each time they start fighting. I can't tell you the number of stops we made, each time making our preteen girls walk further and further. And each time, as they reentered the car, they were fighting about whose fault it was they'd been forced to endure such hardship.

I have lived with fighting kids for thirteen years. I have tried dozens of suggestions of notable authors from Dr. James Dobson to Dr. Joyce Brothers. So what, based on my extensive research and experience, is the surefire way to stop sibling wars? I don't know. I don't think there *are* any surefire answers, but here are some suggestions that may help you survive the battle.

1. Recognize that the worst damage done by kids fighting is the damage done to your nerves. Since you'll probably never get them to stop fighting, insist instead that they not fight in your presence. Let them know how deeply their fighting hurts you and explain that, because of that hurt, you can't bear to watch it or hear it. If fighting breaks out at a meal, ask the combatants to leave. If it starts in a car, the warriors walk until they stop fighting—or, better yet, the parents take a break at an ice cream store, leaving the kids to conduct private peace negotiations in the car. Make it clear that these disciplinary measures are not punishment for fighting—rather, they are a means to stop the fighting in your presence. This approach can reduce the number of battles simply by making fighting so inconvenient. Best of all, it should substantially reduce your stress level because the battles will be taking place where you can't see or hear them.

2. Realize that the verbal sparring is less harmful than it sounds. And that sentence, I have to admit, was almost impossible for me to write even though I know it's true. Fighting kids say things to each other that would cause adults never to speak to each other again. But the kids *do* speak to each other again, often in very friendly tones and soon after the fighting ends, strong evidence that they don't view combat the same way we adults do.

Once I tried to shame my kids into peaceful coexistence. "You don't love each other or you wouldn't fight like this," I accused.

Their reaction was instant and vehement. "We do love each other!" they argued.

Then, after a moment of thought, the youngest piped, "That's the reason we fight so much . . . because we love each other."

I'm not sure how much she understood of what she was saying, but I have come to believe she was absolutely correct. At play and in school with nonsiblings, kids are usually under social pressure not to express their frustrations with each other. Lashing out could destroy fragile friendships and, with them, social status. Kids come home, then, with all that built-up pressure stressing the seams of their growing bodies to the bursting point, only to have a sister or brother "look at them." The explosion is inevitable.

Home is the place where kids can vent those frustrations and know that they will still be accepted and loved. At least, that's what you *want* your home to be. That's why my daughter was probably more right than she realized. Your kids fight because they love each other. It's safe to fight with someone who loves you.

One last suggestion: As you react to your kids' fighting and as you interact with your spouse, make sure you're setting the right example. Bill recently confided that he had seriously scolded his son for the way he spoke to his younger sister. He was particularly disturbed by the demeaning and impatient way he treated her. "We don't talk like that to people," Bill scolded.

"But you talk to mommy like that," his baffled son replied.

At first Bill was defensive, but he quickly realized that his son was right. Even we adults tend to treat those we love with less respect than we would strangers. Be aware of the example you are setting.

We should, of course, strive to teach our children to treat each other with respect. We certainly should work aggressively to discourage any physical abuse in these fights. But for our own good as well as our kids', let's learn not to be gravely disappointed when they fail to live up to our expectations in how they treat their siblings. As they learn to express their anger in more appropriate ways, they will grow out of the fighting stage. Until then, keep calm—and play the peacemaker by insisting that they settle their differences where you can't hear the artillery.

10

What the World Needs Now

Loving Your Kids

A Case for Going the Extra Mile

I was sitting on a beautiful beach in Brownsville, Texas, talking with an agent about the possibility of doing a series of commercial films, when suddenly, out of nowhere, an algae-covered sea monster pitched into my back, knocking me forward. With miles of pristine beach to enjoy, my daughter Taryn (unbeknownst to me) had chosen to wade in a moss-covered sewage lagoon. Draping herself with odoriferous green algae, she had sneaked along the beach looking for me.

Wrapping her smelly, goosebumpy arms tightly around my neck, she pressed her blue, shivering lips to my ear. "You're dead," she proclaimed. "I kill you with love." Then, with a big smack on the cheek, she squealed, "I love you, I love you, I love you!"

The man sitting next to me was not amused. "Could you please ask her to leave until we finish our business?" he grumped.

"Sir," I responded, "our business *is* finished." I had no desire to begin a business relationship with someone so blind to the beauty of a smelly little girl's expressions of love. I spent the rest of the afternoon with the sea monster.

In the sixties, a popular song proclaimed, "What the world needs now is love, sweet love." I wish someone would re-release that song under the title, "What the World Needs More Than Ever Is the Same Love Sweet Love." This chapter explores the desperate need of kids to feel loved, and also examines a model of the kind of unconditional love that can transform you and your family. I'll also suggest some practical ways to express this love daily.

There Is a Love Famine

The evidence that our children live in a love-starved generation is all around us. The second-greatest killer of teenagers in our society is suicide. Many of these kids take their lives because they feel that nobody cares. And for many of them, it's true. Others have moms and dads who care very deeply but don't know how to show it.

Fortunately, suicide is not the solution chosen by most of these love-starved kids—but many of the alternative solutions have serious drawbacks, too. Some seek love outside the home. I see them at camps and conferences, clinging to anyone who will show them a little attention. I see girls in the hallways of our high schools draped all over guys who have offered them the hope of love through a little manipulative attention. You'll find love-starved kids in gangs and occult groups and unhealthy cliques at school—anywhere they feel that they're accepted, that they belong. But a great majority of the kids who feel unloved simply suffer in desperate silence, emotionally hurting and unprepared for the task of loving their own children. They are poised to continue that vicious circle.

The problem is exacerbated by the trends in our society that weaken, rather than strengthen, the family—such as the pervasiveness of divorce and the increase in the number of homes where both parents work—and by a generation of parents who don't know how to express love to their kids. Add to those factors the impersonal, fast-lane pace of our society, and top it off with the truth that teenagers are not the easiest people in the world to love, and you have all the necessary ingredients for loneliness and disaster.

Most parents reading this book would say, "I love my children very much." Unfortunately, even loving homes are often populated by kids who do not *feel* loved.

The adolescent years are particularly difficult for both parents and kids. The complexities of adolescence make it harder for kids to respond to our expressions of love and make our kids more difficult to love. Our cuddly child turns distant and sullen, and we stop making the extra effort to show him love, forgetting that it's during this difficult time that he needs our love most.

There Is a Language Barrier

One of the reasons teenagers don't feel loved is that they speak a different language from their parents. I am no more an expert at being a parent than anyone reading this book, but I do have one advantage over most parents: I have spent a great deal of time listening to thousands of kids and parents. I've had the opportunity to learn the language of both groups. Allow me, in this chapter, to serve as your interpreter.

For example: Many well-meaning parents believe that providing things for their children is an act of love. Indeed it is—in parent language. Your children, however, see it simply as your job. Some of the most loving and emotionally content families in the world are those that don't have all the nice things of life, and some of the saddest, most unloved kids I've met are those who have been given everything. So, if you want your kids to know that you love them, you'll have to do more than just put a roof over their head. You'll have to say it in language that says the same thing to your kids.

A Model for Loving Our Kids

Just because *you* feel love for your kids is no guarantee *they* will feel loved. Your kids need to constantly *hear* the words "I love you" and *see* love demonstrated. In fact, your love for your kids is best demonstrated when you least feel like loving them. The kind of love that makes kids feel loved is *unconditional love*.

Just before he was to be crucified, Jesus gathered his disciples together one last time. He explained that he was not going to be with them much longer. "Where I am going, you cannot come," he said. "A new command I give you." Confused at these hints of Christ's departure, and anxious to understand what was going on, the disciples must have perked up at the mention of this new command. Then Jesus dropped the bomb: "Love one another. As I have loved you, so you must love one another." Then he continued, with words that vibrate in my soul: "By this all men will know that you are my disciples, if you love one another" (John 13:33–35).

Just because *you* feel love for your
kids is no guarantee *they*
will feel loved.

This unconditional love brings hope to broken families. This love can bridge communication gaps that seemed unspannable. Most of all, this love can forever change *your* heart. In this chapter, we'll look at some of the practical ways this love is expressed—but first, let's examine Christ's words carefully, because those who have followed this command have altered history. The power of this kind of love is nothing short of miraculous.

Jesus was speaking to twelve men who had lived and worked together for years, and the first part of his message was that they should love *each other*. Not the rest of the world, not their neighbors, not the people they knew in church—even though his message, by extension, can apply to all those groups as well. His explicit emphasis was that the twelve love each other.

I have lost track of the number of times I have shown more respect and love for strangers than I have for my own family. You can't be selective with this kind of love; you can't skip your own family and love other people. You practice unconditional love where it is the most difficult: with the people you say you love the most.

This message must have disturbed the disciples. It seemed so simple on the surface, but it would be so difficult to apply. It's always harder to unconditionally love people who are close to you because you're so painfully aware of all their faults. Worse, they're aware of yours. Peter responded by offering to die with Jesus: "Lord, why can't I follow you now? I will lay down my life for you" (John 13:37). I've often wondered whether Peter looked around the room at those other twelve men and decided he'd rather die than love those critters. There have certainly been times during my parenthood when I've wanted to throw up my hands and say, "Take me now, God. I'd rather go home now than agonize with these ungrateful bread snappers one more day." Of course those moments are fleeting, but they occur often enough to remind me that it's hard to really show love to those you say you love.

Part two of this command—the aspect that gives it its unique power and difficulty—is the scope of love Jesus wants us to practice. Many times I have wished he had just said, "Love each other." Period. If he had left it there, I could have been satisfied with warm fuzzies, those cozy parental feelings that are common to all of us on occasion. And when those warm, loving feelings weren't there, or when the object of my parental love wasn't being lovable, I would be free to ignore the little brats. But Jesus didn't let us off that easy. He said *I want you to love each other with the same kind of love I showed for you*. That means *unconditional love*. Expecting nothing in return. Ever forgiving. The hard kind of love. Romans 5:8 says, "But God demonstrates his own love for us in this: While we were still sinners, Christ died for us."

Teenagers will intuitively test your
unconditional love with
unlovable behavior.

When we had rejected his love and were in rebellion against him, God chose to love us by sacrificing his son. *That* is unconditional love. And that's the same kind of love he asks us to have for our kids—even when they're rebellious and ungrateful. He doesn't ask us to condone our kids' misbehavior. He asks us to treat them with love even when they're driving us nuts or breaking our heart. Teenagers, especially, will intuitively test your unconditional love with unlovable behavior. Pass that test—affirm your love even when they're at their worst. If you continue to show love even during these difficult times, somewhere deep beneath your child's obnoxious exterior, love will be confirmed.

How, then, can you show Jesus' kind of unconditional love to your child? Read on.

A Strategy for Loving Your Kids

Provide a Secure Home Base

Parents who make no effort to provide shelter and nourishment for their children will be doubted when they say, "I love you." And I'm talking about more than a house and food—I'm talking about a home. Home must be a shelter in a world of storm, a "home base" where a kid is accepted even with all his faults.

If you ever played tag as a child, you remember the frantic efforts to escape those who were trying to tag you. And there was only one safe place, one alternative to simply running until you were exhausted and had to give up. That place was home base. Maybe it was a light pole, maybe it was a bush; wherever it was, it was a haven. Once you caught hold of it, you could no longer be tagged.

Every day of their lives, kids face peer pressure, teasing, and stress whose force we parents have long since forgotten. One of the most loving things we can do is provide a place where our children can rest from those pressures, a place where they are loved and accepted for who they are, rather than ridiculed for who they are not. Unfortunately, some homes are just as tense and hectic as the outside world. Some, in fact, are so stressful that kids seek peace *outside* the home.

A loving, secure home base is an essential foundation for kids to feel loved. But don't expect them to profusely thank you for this provision. They aren't consciously aware of its importance. But they *are* consciously aware of its absence.

EXODUS FROM A TEENAGER'S ROOM.

Without it, their emotional survival is difficult. Many parents say to their kids, "Haven't I worked my fingers to the bone to put a roof over your head and provide a place for you to call home?" Then they're surprised when their kids respond with blank stares, confusion, or—depending on the courage of the child—a disgusted roll of the eyeballs. Kids take their safe home base for granted—until it isn't there.

Is your house a home base?

Say the Magic Words

It's like the woman who told her marriage counselor that she didn't feel loved by her husband. Indignantly, her husband responded, "I told her I loved her when I married her. If I change my mind, I'll let her know."

This man didn't know it, but his wife needed to *hear* the words. And so do your kids. Say the words, "I love you." Every day. But don't expect your kids to react with grateful acknowledgment or to return the favor, especially if they're teenagers. Kids of that age just don't do that.

"I love you," I say to my oldest daughter.

"Me too," she responds.

"Well, say it to me, then," I insist.

"I did," she says.

"Watch my lips," I say. "I. Love. You."

"Me too," she repeats.

Of course she loves me. But *saying* the words doesn't seem important to her, even though she needs to *hear* them. In *How to Really Love Your Teenager*, Ross Campbell tells of calling his son on the phone specifically to remind him how much he loved him. And after his son had heard that message, he responded with, "Great, Dad, but what did you call me for?"

So if there's not likely to be any demonstrative response when you say "I love you," why do it? Because every time you say it, deep inside your child, another brick is laid in the foundation of love. And whether your children acknowledge it or not, your words are filed as evidence that you really do care. Make it a point to say those words every day.

Praise Positive Attitudes and Good Behavior

Verbal praise and encouragement are also important in expressing love. I'm continually discovering the importance of this with my kids. It's so easy to always harp on the things they do wrong and never verbally praise them for the things they do right. But even a lack of criticism is never interpreted as an expression of love. When a child responds positively even in the smallest way to your expectations, lavish them with praise.

After a seminar, one parent said to me, "The world isn't going to praise my kids for doing what's expected—so why should I?" That's precisely the reason you should. The world does not love your children, but you do. When you praise them even for simple compliance to your rules or for the smallest positive indications of character in their lives, you set yourself apart from the rest of the world. You show that you really do care. Praise and encouragement register high on the love scale in the mind of your child.

Get Physical

Humans are designed to express love through physical contact. Unfortunately, we often give our pets more of this kind of love than we do our children. Especially older children. It's easier to cuddle a cute little kid who affectionately returns your love than it is to hug a silent, moody teenager who doesn't respond or even resists your expressions. Don't give up.

For a couple of years, Traci was reluctant to hug me. She would patronizingly allow our foreheads to touch and pat me on the back. Then, for some unknown, unseen reason, that period ended, and suddenly she began responding with the affectionate bear hugs I like. Many kids reach an age at which, for a period of time, they are uncomfortable with physical displays of affection. Don't force it. You may have to settle for a clap on the back or a touch on the arm as you pass. By the way—I've never met a teenager who liked to have his or her hair ruffled. I knew a boy whose uncle did it every time they met, and it drove the boy nuts. Finally, in desperation, he did it back to his uncle—and shifted the man's hairpiece about three inches to the left. He quickly discovered that his uncle didn't like it either.

As late as the 1920s, there was an alarming death rate in U.S. orphanages. After much study, it was discovered that what these children needed was to be held. The death rate dropped dramatically when the workers were instructed to hold the babies, stroke them, and talk to them. Humans literally can't survive without being touched. Alan Loy McGinnis tells this story in his book *The Friendship Factor*:

> The young desperately crave physical affection. Howard Maxwell of Los Angeles is a man in tune with his times. So when his four-year-old daughter Melinda acquired a fixation for "The Three Little Pigs" and demanded that he read it to her night after night, Mr. Maxwell, very pleased with himself, tape-recorded the story. When Melinda next asked for it, he simply switched on the playback. This worked for a couple of nights, but then one evening Melinda pushed the storybook at her father. "Now honey," he said, "you know how to turn on the recorder." "Yes," said Melinda, "but I can't sit on its lap."[1]

Don't stop touching your kids. Even during the years Traci was uncomfortable with hugs, she was always glad to wrestle—a father-daughter activity we had begun back when the girls were small. Back in those days, they would try to get me pinned to the floor so I couldn't move. They thought it was great fun when I would throw them off like wet rags. Why would a girl who was hesitant to give me a big hug stand for such prolonged physical contact? Because it was an acceptable way for her to have contact with her dad. Touching communicates love. Kids need some kind of physical expression of love. Find their comfort zone and touch them often.

A word of caution. If you haven't been physical with your children up to this point, don't close this book and throw your arms around the first kid that walks through the door, or you may be in for a painful surprise. Start with the more subtle and less threatening gestures of love; in time, your kids may open up to more demonstrative expression.

It's unfortunate that we live in a society that reads sexual connotations into almost all expressions of love, parental touching included. It's vitally important that you don't color any of your parent/child contact with this damaging baggage.

There is a big difference between the crisp hug of a loving mother or father and the lingering embrace of romance. A parental kiss is a peck on the lips or an extra firm smack on the cheek or forehead. Be careful—but don't let your fear of being misunderstood keep you from finding a way to touch your child in love.

Give Your Kids the Time of Day

One of the most important expressions of love involves neither words nor physical contact. It's your time. Once again, don't expect lavish thanks for this demonstration of love, but unless you're willing to spend time with your kids, they may question your love even though you care very much.

In Zig Ziglar's book *How to Raise Positive Kids in a Negative World,* he includes this heading: "Love is spelled T I M E."[2] That says it. Few things demonstrate your love to your kids more than that. When kids are asked, "How do you know that your parents love you?" time is almost always included in their response. You don't hear, "Because they touch me. Because they work hard. Because they give me rules to help build my character. Because they praise me when I do right." Even though these are important expressions of love, your kids aren't as conscious of them. But they *are* conscious of the time you give them.

Love is spelled T I M E.

We've all heard this: "It isn't the *quantity* of time that's important—its the *quality* of time." What a copout. I don't believe it for a moment, and neither do kids. Try spending only five or ten minutes a day with your spouse over the next month, but make it quality time—and see what happens. On second thought, don't. After a few days, you'd probably find your luggage sitting on the front porch.

Your kids need quantity *and* quality time. According to a 1989 Focus on the Family bulletin, "The average child spends only 25 minutes a week in close interaction with his father."

That may be a generous estimate. Although mothers statistically spend more, it is often not quality time—much of it is spent scolding, giving instructions, or making demands.

> Parents spend far more time than they realize supervising their children: Where are you going? What time will you be back? Wash your hair. Don't slurp your soup. Hurry up or you'll miss the bus. And as a result, they spend much less time than they realize actually interacting with them. For a study on parent/child interaction, a team of New York psychologists asked a group of middle class fathers to estimate the amount of time they spent playing with their year-old infants each day. The average answer was fifteen to twenty minutes. But when the fathers were actually observed, the time was shockingly less. The mean number of interactions per day was 2.7 and the number of seconds for each involvement rounded out to thirty-eight. Less than a minute a day for so much as a koochy-koo.[3]

If both parents work, it's that much harder to find the time you need to be spending with your kids. *The Los Angeles Times* reported in September of 1989 that:

> By some estimates, more than 40% of children under the age of 13—somewhere between one million and six million kids—go home to an empty house after school. "These estimates may be low," suggests the researcher, "because parents may be reluctant to admit that their children have no adult supervision."

Josh McDowell says:

> Adult contact is also limited by the busyness of the modern American family. With all the activities of parents and children—lessons and meetings and practices and games—it's difficult for the typical family to have meals together, much less significant discussions or even just plain fun as a family.
>
> Interaction between parents and children is limited even further by the still growing phenomenon of both parents working outside the home. This means more and more school age children are coming home to empty houses—the "latch key kids." Rather than interacting with a parent during the after school hours, these youngsters have television or friends as companions. Fifty years ago, the average child had three to four hours a day of interaction with parents or extended family

members. Today's child has only about 15 minutes of interaction with parents a day. And twelve of those minutes are in a setting of critique, instruction or criticism.[4]

To complicate matters further, as your kids approach their teen years they don't need *less* of your time—they need more. And to top it all off, they act like they don't want to spend *any* time with you. Just about the time your kids get old enough to make good companions, they choose to spend most of their time with their friends.

Very young children aren't the most stimulating conversationalists, and it's often frustrating to try to involve them in many of the things we enjoy (fishing, shopping, working on cars) that older children and teens are capable of enjoying right along with us. Still, spending time with your kids when they are young is an investment that will pay off when they are older. The story is told of the old man who found his grown son's childhood journal. As he looked at the entries, out of curiosity he compared them with the entries from his own journal for the same days. One entry was particularly telling. On that day he had taken his young son fishing. The entry in the old man's journal read, "Wasted the whole day fishing." In his son's journal, he found this entry for the same day: "Went fishing with my dad. Best day of my life."

**You'll never *find* the time to spend
with your kids. You must
plan for it.**

Our lives are busy. How do we find the time to spend with our son or daughter? The same way we find the time for the other important things in our lives: We plan for it. My children have access to my calendar. Birthdays, special school events, and other times when they want me to be present can be marked with a big red X. Those times are sacred. They are just as important to me as a high-paying booking with a large corporation. You will never *find* the time to spend with your kids. You must *plan* for it.

Besides these planned times, be available for emergencies—those times, for instance, when your child just needs to talk. Talking with your children is so important that almost nothing should keep you from responding when they ask for your time. One of the reasons many kids stop talking to their parents during adolescence is that those parents are always too busy to give them full attention. Usually, your kids only want a few minutes. What's more important than a few minutes that will communicate love to your child? Work can be finished later. Television can certainly wait. The newspaper won't rot while you take the time to talk with your child. And their knowledge that you love them enough to give them your time carries weight in the love column of their life.

Spend Quality Time

Quality time is when your kids have your undivided attention. You can't communicate love from behind a newspaper or with your eyes glued to the TV. Stop what you are doing. Sit down, establish eye contact, and listen.

I don't believe most politicians care about me. I have had my hand clasped by dozens of these buzzards, and never once were they looking at me or paying attention to what I said. Usually, they were looking over my shoulder to see whether there were someone more important they needed to greet. Often, during that brief moment when the candidate stood before me, shaking my hand, I've tried to express my concern about some issue of importance to me—and he has interrupted with a canned answer that didn't even fit the question as he smiled and waved at someone else in the crowd. In those moments, I felt embarrassed and used.

Yet we often treat our children in just that way. Instead, give them your undivided, focused attention. And if you avoid (as much as possible) spending those rare bits of time talking about obedience and discipline, you'll find that your kids will want to talk to you more often. Save discipline for another time. *Quality time is when you listen more than you talk.* Your ears communicate love much better than your lips. Search for the hot buttons that unleash your children's tongues, and then listen. Sometimes you'll have to sit through a lot of silence before they open up, but when they do, you have struck gold, so behave accordingly. This is the time for loving. And in this case, loving is the willingness to listen.

Many parents, through necessity, understand the importance of quality time. Some of them, because of divorce, live in homes other than the homes of their children. Their time with their kids is restricted to a few weeks or days a year. Other parents, forced by economic necessity to work, have little time to spend with their children. For several years, I too worked so much I didn't make time to be with my children. I had to rethink my priorities. One of the wisest (and most difficult) decisions I've ever made was to cut my travel schedule by more than a hundred days a year. That decision has cost me thousands of dollars over the past fifteen years, but it has been worth every penny. I believe it saved my family.

Please don't underestimate the importance of spending time with your kids. Make every minute count. There is so little time available to influence the lives of our children, and that time is worth much more than a few more dollars of disposable income, a new car, or an upgraded standard of living. Protect your times together. Clear your schedule so that, when you're with your kids, you're *with* them—they have your undivided attention.

Plan activities for that time that you both enjoy. An environment of fun can go a long way toward getting you off on the right foot. Be careful not to fill this time with adultisms and informational nagging. When any parent/child event turns into a marathon of instruction and criticism, the chance for real bonding and enjoyment disappears. Sometimes, just having fun is all the agenda you need. Relax. Enjoy the company of your child—and watch for opportunities to communicate.

When the opportunity to listen and communicate on deeper levels arises, make the most of it. Make yourself vulnerable; encourage them to talk. Listen to their frustrations even if some of them are vented in your direction. Say the magic words during these special times. If need be, take your child's face in your hands and say, "I love you."

Don't be disappointed if your "quality time" doesn't turn out the way you thought it would. We often set our expectations for these times too high. If you expect an emotionally gratifying response from your child, you'll probably be disappointed. Kids are terrible at meeting the emotional needs of their parents. (They weren't designed for that purpose, and it isn't their responsibility.) Plan to give as much of yourself as possible, knowing that even though you'll get from your child little visible confirmation of the value of your time, that value is registering deep within your child's soul.

Express Love in the Little Things

Most of have been tricked into believing that love is communicated only when tumultuous emotions are unleashed or expensive gifts are exchanged. But love is communicated in little things: A note of support in a lunch box or tucked into a school book. A little help with a chore when your kids aren't expecting it. A special lunch or dinner with just you and your child. These little expressions of love carry more weight than we realize.

The other day I made arrangements to pick Taryn up at school. We picked up a couple of submarine sandwiches and had a picnic lunch at the park. No earth-shaking subjects were discussed; no discipline was handed out. We just spent an hour together laughing at the antics of some ducks. Later I found out that our date had meant enough to Taryn that she had told many of her friends about it. I also found out that her friends were envious; they expressed a desire to have a similar date with their fathers.

Little things mean a lot. One day, years ago, I was sitting at home reading on my day off. The door to a storage closet was open, and the vacuum cleaner caught my eye. At that time in my life, I wasn't much of a help around the house, but for some reason that day I decided to vacuum. I learned many things that day. I discovered that our cat was terrified of the vacuum cleaner. (I cornered her and vacuumed her anyway.) I also discovered that there are many things the vacuum won't pick up. Toothpicks, lint, and rubberbands are almost hopeless. I ended up taking off all the hoses and bringing these items from all over the house to feed to it. But the discovery that motivated me to vacuum the whole house was the stripes the vacuum made. When I would go one way, it would shade the carpet dark; when I went the other way, it would shade it light! I was so fascinated that I striped the whole house. Then I went the other direction and made a checkerboard pattern.

I was admiring my artwork when Diane came home from work. When she walked in the door, I made the most important discovery of all. Her mouth dropped open as she observed the neatly vacuumed rooms. Slowly the groceries slipped to the floor. "Thank you!" she cried, launching herself into my arms. In the midst of the kissing and fooling around, we lost our balance and broke a coffee table. It was wonderful! She read my vacuuming as an expression of love. I vacuum a lot more often now.

Look for little ways to help your kids, little ways to express your love. Because the little things really do mean a lot.

Love Them by Loving Each Other

One of the best ways to show love to your children is to show love to your husband or wife. Kids who see their parents love each other feel loved themselves. Don't hide all those little love pats and kisses from your kids. The younger ones may wrinkle up their nose and complain when they see your displays of affection; teenagers may appear to be on the verge of throwing up. Don't stop—you are communicating love to your children as well as to your spouse.

One of the best ways to show love to
your children is to show love to
your husband or wife.

In his wonderful book *Talking with Your Kids About Love, Sex and Dating*, Barry St. Clair recalls this incident:

We stood in the kitchen smooching. Johnathan walked in and exclaimed, "Gross me out." Before he turned to leave, he smiled. . . . Our children will sense the love between us when they see physical affection. They learn how to express affection from their parents.[5]

How does expressing love for your spouse also express love for your children? One of the greatest fears faced by children is fear of the breakup of the home. Constant strife between mom and dad, or the lack of affection between the two of you, threatens the security of that home base and subtly brings your love into question. You probably don't love your children any less when there's strife between you and your spouse, but they *feel* less loved. And in some families, parents have allowed their marriage to deteriorate as they have thrown all their effort into meeting the needs of their children. If you allow this to happen, you threaten one of your children's greatest needs of all: The need to see the positive expressions of love that emanate from a secure marriage.

One of the most effective things you can do to meet the needs of your children is to work hard at keeping your marriage strong. Even though your children may never verbally express that need, it is essential to their emotional health. It is one of the strongest confirmations of your love.

As you seek God's strength to love your kids unconditionally, an interesting thing happens: *You* will begin to change. You will find that this kind of loving is habit-forming. Practicing this kind of love brings peace to your soul like little else can. And this kind of love does not go unnoticed. Although you may not receive verbal affirmation from the people toward whom you're expressing unconditional love, the people around you are seeing in your life a demonstration of the power of God. Jesus said, "By this all men will know that you are my disciples, if you love one another." Such testimony to his power in your life lays a solid foundation for a possible change in your kids' lives. Loving your children unconditionally may be the hardest task for a parent. But nothing you do as a parent will be a more effective testimony of God's power in your life, nor provide greater evidence of your love to your child.

11

Working Yourself Out of a Job

Helping Your Kids Grow Toward Independence

I had never stopped to consider the end result of being a parent until Traci entered junior high. I took her to school that day. As we pulled up to the school, my heart was doing flip-flops. I didn't want to drop her off here. *Evil Junior High*—it was written right on the building. What a difference from the warm, innocent, nurturing atmosphere of grade school. There were kids entering that building with hairstyles that could cause bodily injury. A small group of kids were gathered at one end of the property smoking who knows what, and a number of teachers were gathered at the other end of the property doing the same thing.

Against all my instincts as a parent, I left her in this new and dangerous place and went to my office. I was worthless. I counted the hours until I could rescue my baby from that institution of iniquity. When the final bell rang at the end of the school day, I was already standing just outside the main doors, waiting. A tidal wave of kids swept past me, and suddenly I felt an emotion I had never felt before: fear that my daughter would be embarrassed because I was there. I looked around; there were no other parents in sight. All of them were hiding in the safety of their cars. Was I acting like a "geek" by standing here? (*Geek* is a word used by kids to describe one who acts in an uncool, unsophisticated, geek-like manner. According to kids, most adults are already geeks or studying for geekdom.) I wasn't willing to take that chance. I moved over to the door where all the teachers were coming out. They looked at me as though I were a heroin dealer looking for a score. If there's anything worse than looking like a geek to your kid's friends, it's proving you're a geek to your kid's teachers. I retreated to the safety of my car.

I saw Traci immediately; she burst from the school with a gaggle of friends. (A gaggle is a small group of gigglers.) In the midst of excited conversation, she was obviously looking for me. A tentative toot of the horn did the trick. She broke from her friends, ran to my car, and dived through the open window. She hugged and kissed me and then, voice trembling with excitement, she bubbled, "Daddy, it's wonderful! Can I walk home with my new friends?"

"Of course," I responded. Before the words were even out of my mouth, she broke away from the car to run back to her friends, squealing with delight. I made it about a block before I pulled the car over and wept uncontrollably. (Definite geek-like behavior.) For some reason, that simple incident made me suddenly aware that my "baby" was quickly becoming an independent young woman, soon capable of making it on her own. A chapter of her life had closed, and it could never be reopened. In this new chapter, she would not need the same Daddy she had needed before.

The moment the doctor cuts the umbilical cord, kids begin a mad dash for freedom. They don't make much headway at first, because they can't move or communicate real well, but through the effective use of their lungs, they make it clear that their wishes don't always line up with yours. Later, when they learn the word no, they remove any doubt.

This drive for independence intensifies as kids approach adolescence and struggle to control their own lives. It can be a confusing and difficult time for a parent—the child who has always been compliant and obedient is suddenly fighting you at every turn. The little kid who needed you so desperately for so many years, the one who clung to your leg like a growth, now prefers to be on his own. Some children don't even want to be seen with you. After thirteen or fourteen years of parenting, your mind is already gone and you probably feel that you lack the energy, wisdom, and patience to cope with this insistence on independence.

For me, this period is by far the most challenging aspect of parenting—but also the most rewarding. The struggles we have faced in our family as we have addressed our daughters' drive for independence have drawn us closer together than at any other time in our lives. Here are some ideas that have been helpful to us.

Recognize That the Drive for Independence Is Normal

Understand, first of all, that it is part of God's plan that your children eventually leave you and start their own families. Matthew 19:5 says, "For this reason a man will leave his father and mother and be united to his wife, and the two will become one flesh." Notice that there is only room for so much flesh. Mom and Dad are not included at this point. By this time, we should have worked ourselves out of a job.

Second, we must recognize that it is our responsibility to help our kids grow toward independence so that, when they reach their late teens, they are capable of making decisions and accepting responsibility in an adult fashion. Many parents find themselves unconsciously doing just the opposite—fighting their kids' move toward independence. But let's be honest: Accepting adolescent behavior as normal and helping a kid move toward independence is a lot like walking a narrow bridge while hostile natives throw spears at you. Just at the age kids require more freedom, they are surrounded by opportunities that can ruin their lives. To make it more difficult, they may show little evidence of being able to handle responsibility, they are subject to peer pressure as never before, and their bizarre behavior can make you want to wring their little necks before they ever reach adulthood. We parents must nevertheless encourage our children toward independence, not away from it, and if we don't, we're not doing our job.

Recognize the Symptoms

I think every parent is sometimes convinced that the weirdness that takes place during their children's adolescent years is unique to their family. Many times, after a seminar, a parent will accuse me of spying on their home. They are relieved when I assure them that I didn't, because for the first time they realize that other families face the same problems. Once they recognize the symptoms of this widespread "independence disease," they are better able to cope with it. See if these symptoms sound familiar.

Dr. Jekyll and Mr. Hyde

One day your sweet little kid skips to school humming the mulberry bush song, and that night the same kid comes home acting like Mr./Ms. Hyde. It seems to happen overnight, and once they've acquired the capacity for this kind of behavior, they can switch in a second from acting like a full-grown adult to acting like a one-year-old with a loaded diaper. An adolescent is like a butterfly emerging from a cocoon, except he keeps crawling back in. Throughout these difficult years, the adult and the child will alternately show their heads—and we parents must be prepared to meet the needs of both.

Ross Campbell explains this behavior in his book *How to Really Love Your Teenager*:

> Teenagers are children emotionally. To illustrate this let's look at how a teenager is like a two-year-old. Both a teenager and a two-year-old have drives for independence and both have emotional tanks. Each will strive for independence, using the energy from the emotional tank. When the emotional tank has run dry, the teenager and the two-year-old will do the same thing—return to the parent for a refill so they can again strive for independence. . . . The child must repeatedly return to the parent to have his emotional tank refilled in order to continue his quest for independence. This is exactly what happens with the early adolescent. He may use different means of exerting his drive for independence (and sometimes in disturbing and upsetting ways). He needs the energy from his emotional tank to do this. And where does he get his emotional tank refilled? Right! From his parents. A teenager will strive for indepen-

dence in typical adolescent ways—doing things by himself, going places without family, testing parental rules. But he will eventually run out of emotional gasoline and come back to the parent for emotional maintenance—for a refill. This is what we want, as parents of teenagers. We want our adolescent to be able to come to us for emotional maintenance when he needs it.[1]

Ross's explanation helped me to understand some of the strange behavior of my kids, but it also left me with a formidable challenge: If my kid is going to come back to me for emotional support, I must be capable and willing to give that support. And that is yet another reason that we must continue to allow God to change our attitude and our responses to our children, keeping them within the context of unconditional love. If we don't, we may begin to react defensively, punishing our children's adventurous probes into independence by refusing to refill their tanks. That refusal can have tragic consequences. If your children can't get their emotional tanks refilled by you, they may be driven to unknowledgeable, unreliable, or even unsavory sources for emotional filling.

An adolescent is like a butterfly
emerging from a cocoon,
except he keeps crawling back in.

Providing your child's emotional refilling sounds easy on paper, but it can be difficult in real life. For instance, I was deeply hurt and shocked one day when I said to the fruit of my loins, the object of my love, the focus of my toil—Traci— "Guess what, honey? We're going to spend the weekend in the mountains."

She responded by tipping her head to one side and rolling her eyes disgustedly. "Is this going to one of those family things?" she asked.

Fourteen years of devotion, hundreds of hours of anxiety, countless sleepless nights, not to mention thousands of dollars spent providing for her material needs all seemed to be flushed right down the old commode with that one response. The blood vessels in my neck began to swell, and a small trickle of drool escaped the corner of my mouth. But I controlled myself. We talked further, and it became clear that her reply was not a condemnation of our family. Rather, it was a poorly phrased, badly timed expression of independence.

Unless your self-esteem is in great shape and your own reservoir of unconditional love has been filled by God's grace, you may mistake these clumsy expressions as an ungrateful rejection of everything you have ever done for the child, and respond accordingly. But because Traci and I have worked hard to keep our communication lines open and operative, I was able to see that her response was not an attack on me or on our family. Rather, it was a request, and I responded to that request with compromise. Traci went with us to the mountains, allowing me the serenity of having my family together— but she brought a friend, allowing her a security blanket of independence.

A Focus on Friends

This desperate need to be with friends of their own choosing is another key demonstration of your children's growing independence. I'll admit that I had to work hard not to resent my daughters' friends. Just when they reached the age where they could be delightful companions for me, they chose these vagabonds instead.

Teenagers feel an almost desperate need to build at least part of their world completely independent from their parents, and their circle of friends becomes that world. The tough balancing act for parents is to allow teens that freedom and yet avoid having them withdraw totally from the family. But you can achieve that balance by concentrating on two strategies.

First—and vitally important—plan time with the family. Teenagers resist family time because it takes them away from their friends. After all, who knows—the whole world could come to an end while they're out of contact. Allowing my daughters to touch base by telephone once or twice during a family weekend reassures them that their friendships are still intact and that nobody crucial has died. Don't give in to the relentless pressure from your teens to spend all their time with their friends. And don't be discouraged by the sullen attitudes of teenagers forced to go on these boring excursions. They need these times more than ever; it's just that they aren't aware of it. Plan times for the family to be together, and make it fun for them to participate.

Second, it's important to treat your kids' friends with respect. If you make those young people feel welcome in your home, you may be *blessed* with a houseful of kids that are not your own. It's true that a parade of teenagers through your castle can be trying, but it has some wonderful advantages. For one, it allows you to assess the character of the people your kids are choosing as friends; for another, it centers their activities where you can keep track of what's going on. I have grown to love many of my daughters' friends, and I'm always happy, believe it or not, to have a quiet evening disrupted by their rowdy playing in our home.

A Struggle for Control

One of the most difficult aspects of parenting kids who are pushing for independence is knowing how much control to exert over their lives. When they were small, the limits you set were probably fairly strict as you sought to teach the principles that would enrich their lives. But as they grew older, you broadened the limits within which you allowed them to roam.

When your child was a baby, you limited his world to a crib and your arms. As he got a little older, he was allowed full run of a play area. Eventually he was wobbling about the house investigating electrical outlets, stove controls, and toilet bowls. As his physical abilities grew, he grew more and more independent—and frequently needed new sets of guidelines to match the increasing size of his world. And each new set of guidelines made the challenges of parenting that much tougher. Even so, the process seemed fairly smooth and manageable through the elementary years. And then came junior high. Suddenly, you needed to establish guidelines to govern a whole new realm of activities that were a quantum leap from everything that had come before. The old rules that covered the cookie jar and crossing the street just don't apply

EVERY FATHER'S NIGHTMARE!

to this brave new world. Everything up to this point was just kid stuff. Now we're dealing with real, live adult issues.

Kids who've been given a lot of freedom during their childhood years suddenly feel cramped by the new limits set on their life. They feel as though they're being treated like children again. Which is one of the reasons early adolescence brings so many conflicts: Just as the urges for revolution and independence are at their peak, new restrictions are needed.

It's best to prepare for this change ahead of time. Sit down with your late-elementary-age child and explain that, within a few years, a whole new frontier of responsibility is going to open to him. Share your plan to establish rather strict limits at the beginning of this adventure and work together to build responsibility and trust that will allow him more freedom. Make sure he knows that the new limitations will not be punishment for past sins, but rather protection and preparation for new freedoms.

Your kids need to understand that you want to work *together* to help them achieve independence—not to control and restrict them for the rest of their life. Beginning with fairly strict limitations gives you plenty of room to loosen up as your kids prove themselves responsible. I said it's important for your kids to understand this, and it's important for you to remember it as well. Balancing responsibility and restriction isn't easy; understanding that one of your major roles during this time is to help your child move toward freedom and independence puts the job into a perspective that may make some of your decisions easier. Without that perspective, you'll feel as if all your time is spent fighting for control.

If your kids are already teenagers and you didn't prepare them to understand your actions when they were younger, all is not lost. Sit down now and talk with them. Let them express their frustrations; then explain your goal. Work together to decide where you can compromise and where you'll have to agree to disagree. The important thing is to let your kids know your motives for the restrictions you set and your intentions of giving them the opportunity to gain trust and freedom.

I found myself in this position with my older daughter. At fourteen years old, she asked to go to a nightclub. Many of her friends attended a local dance spot that opened its doors to kids one night a week. Although no alcohol was sold inside, there were many drunken fights in the parking lot, and the police were often called to break up disturbances on the property. I wasn't excited about that club, and I wasn't excited about her getting into the nightclub scene in the first place.

She turned on all the burners when I told her she couldn't go. "I've never done anything to make you distrust me!" she cried. "You keep saying that as I get older I can have more freedom, but you *never* let me do the things I want!" Sound familiar?

We sat down. I explained why I didn't feel this was a good place for her to go. None of my reasons made any sense to her. I told her that I had complete confidence in her, but that I was unwilling to put her in situations where she could be hurt or tempted beyond her control. None of that made sense either. But she finally began to see some hope for her future when I suggested that we have lunch together and talk about alternative areas where I could give her more freedom and opportunities to prove that she was becoming more responsible. In the end, she readily traded her nightclub request for several other more wholesome opportunities to prove trustworthiness. Within a few days, she seemed to have forgotten all about the nightclub. She has never asked to go again. On last night's local news, the announcer discussed new attempts to close it down because of the constant disturbances there. We watched that news report together, and although I was tempted, the words *I told you so* never escaped my lips.

Even the best of kids will push your rules to the limit during their run for independence. They have the ability to make you wonder whether you are the most cruel person in the universe for even suggesting that they should have rules. You may doubt they will ever recover emotionally; you may be tempted to give in. Don't. If your motivation is on track and if the guidelines you have set are consistent, stick to your guns. Many of the crises that seem so important fade into insignificance in a few days. If you had heard the heartrending pleas Traci presented to persuade me to let her go to that nightclub, you'd have thought her life depended on going. Within days, it wasn't even worth discussion.

And simply waiting a few days is an excellent way to handle some of the conflicts that will come as your kids strive for independence. Taryn came home one day and announced that she and three of her girlfriends were going to Aspen to ski for the weekend. The brother (seventeen years old) of one of the girls was going to drive them there and serve as chaperon. All of this was presented as if it were a common and reasonable request. When I said no, tears flooded the room; it was as though I had just condemned her to social death. *You don't trust me! What will my friends think! I never get to do anything!* I got the whole repertoire. Fortunately, there wasn't a parent among these girls dumb enough to let their preteen drive a hundred miles to go skiing for the weekend with a teenage boy as chaperon. The deal fell apart of its own accord. The tears dried up as though nothing had ever happened when Taryn realized that she wasn't going to miss the big event— there would be no big event to miss. What seems like the most important event of the century will often fade into historical insignificance if you give it a little time.

Use This Time to Build Trust

It is during the push for independence that one of the most important characteristics of all relationships can be built: trust. Mutual trust between parent and teenager is a cherished goal that should be pursued with diligence. Teach your child to value trust as though it were gold. One way to do this is by rewarding trustworthy behavior with grown-up responsibility. Kids searching for independence love to be treated like adults, so they'll be glad to be given more responsibility. But be careful. The foundation for trust must be built slowly (much more slowly, no doubt, than your teenager would like to see it built) and carefully. And that process can be short-circuited if you give your teenagers more responsibility than they are capable of handling. It's safest if both parties keep the goal, as well as the steps that must be taken to get there, in clear view.

For example: The first time your kids stay home without a

baby-sitter, they'll be ecstatic and you'll be a nervous wreck. Let them know that this is a test. If they behave responsibly, other more exciting adult responsibilities can be theirs soon. But be sure to define responsible behavior: The house must not be trashed. No parties, no friends over. (Having a friend over when parents are gone may eventually be one of the privileges granted when your teens have demonstrated that they can be trusted.) Don't leave the house. Finish your chores and homework.

When the reward is trust and increased freedom, you would be surprised what teens are capable of. Tell the neighbors what's going on; enlist their help to keep an eye on things for safety's sake. When you get home, if all the conditions have been met, the house is still standing, and siblings have not been beaten beyond recognition, lavish your kids with praise and let them know that they will have other opportunities to demonstrate even more responsibility.

In fairness, you should also let your kids know right from the beginning, before any test, how hard it is to rebuild trust that has been broken. Make it clear that many privileges that have taken a long time to gain can be lost in one irresponsible moment. Trust is fragile—and that means that you should be as protective of the trust your teenagers build as they are. Be forewarned: They *will* make some mistakes. They'll become very discouraged if every mistake in judgment sends them back to zero. Instead, let those mistakes become teaching tools. Lying, outright deceit, and disobedience are trust killers—let your kids know the damage that these behaviors can cause. Inappropriate behavior and poor decisions are typical of teenagers; they simply mean that some maturing and learning need to take place. But if they keep recurring, they may also indicate that your child is not yet ready for the amount of responsibility you have given him. Give him a chance to show better judgment before you take away responsibility. Whenever possible, use these errors of judgment to discuss and teach the appropriate response.

There are three levels of trust. Total trust is the highest level; that should be your ultimate goal as a parent. Total trust is achieved when your child is obedient to the guidelines you have set, truthful about what goes on, and mature enough to avoid making errors of judgment. You can trust such a child in new situations without supervision and allow him or her expanded responsibility. Limited trust describes kids who are honest and obedient but have not matured enough to exercise consistently good judgment. These children need to know that they are trusted, but that you will continue to exercise some supervision until they can make mature decisions. At the third level, trust is lacking altogether. No child should be put in this category simply because of judgment errors. Deceit, lying, and purposeful disobedience are the behaviors that utterly destroy a parent's trust. And once trust has been destroyed, it can only be rebuilt by carefully starting from near the beginning, demonstrating once again that the child can be trusted in little things.

Trust is a two-way street. You can't expect a child to value trustworthiness if she has parents who can't be trusted. Let your own moral standards be a model for your children. No child will much value a parent's trust after they discover that that parent has been intentionally deceiving them. You can't engage in extramarital affairs, dishonest business practices, or substance abuse and expect a kid to listen to your lecture on integrity and trustworthiness.

While we visited in a home one evening, the phone rang several times. Each time it was answered by one of the kids in the home, and each time the parents asked the children to tell the caller they weren't home. Later that evening, our discussion came round to parenting. These parents lamented that their kids lied to them all the time. I was surprised—these parents seemed blind to the fact that they had helped teach their kids to lie.

Even in the small things, model in your own life the quality that you expect in your children. Don't give them a reason to mistrust you. Talk about the importance of trust often.

Keep even the smallest promises that you make to your children. Parents sometimes feel free to break promises if they don't seem important. But to a kid, *all* promises are important. If you say you'll play ball later in the day, be sure to follow through. If you don't keep your promises, don't expect your kids to keep theirs. If something happens making it impossible to play ball, explain what happened, apologize, and set another time. And make sure it doesn't happen again for a long time.

Admit your shortcomings and mistakes; show that you're working to correct them. Kids won't mistrust a parent who's not perfect, but they will mistrust a parent who lies and covers up to make people think he *is* perfect.

Be consistent in your discipline. Even though they fight the rules, kids find security and confidence in consistent discipline. If one time you respond with anger and punishment over a specific behavior and the next time you ignore it, your kids may lose respect for all your rules and distrust your word.

The other night I was watching television, and an ad came on. "Do you have a teenager who is moody?" the voice droned. "Do they break the rules you set and spend most of their time with friends? Does it seem that they are moving further away from the family? If this sounds like your teenager, call Vision Hospital—we can help."

I wanted to say, if this sounds like your teenager, make a cup of coffee and relax—you have a normal teenager. Of course, *extremes* of any of those symptoms would be reason to seek help. But in normal doses, they are all just signs of the drive for independence. It isn't always fun living with an adolescent, but it's always challenging. For years I listened to people warn, "Wait till your kids reach those teenage years. It's horrible." I refused to expect it to be horrible. And I wouldn't trade the times I am experiencing with my two headstrong teenage girls struggling for independence for any other period in their lives. Working through these times has enabled our family to love each other more than we have at any other point in our lives.

The teenage struggle for independence is normal. Your role as a parent is not to fight it, but rather to recognize its symptoms and help your kid grow to be a healthy, independent adult.

In short—it's your job to work yourself out of a job.

12

Remembering the Good Times

Creating a Museum of Wonderful Memories

Memory! What a gift of God. And what a tragedy at times. Memory can be of horrible things one wants to forget, coming at times like a nightmare trembling of horror, or memory can be of wonderful things one enjoys living and reliving. Memory can bring sudden understanding later in life. . . .

What is a family meant to be? Among other things, I personally have always felt it is meant to be a museum of memories—a collection of carefully preserved memories and a realization that day by day memories are being chosen for our museum . . . and that time can be made to have double value by recognizing that what is done today will be tomorrow's memory.[1]

I hate to admit this, but one day not long ago I got lost within blocks of my home. You would think that after living in the same place for seventeen years, that would be impossible, but I did it. My mind was preoccupied with some problem, and I made a couple of turns without paying attention and lost track of the familiar landmarks. When my mind emerged from the fog, I was disoriented. At first I thought that I was near my home, but when I didn't see anything I recognized, I began to doubt that I was even in the right city.

If you've ever experienced this, you know how unsettling it can be. I sat at an intersection, not knowing which way to turn. Suddenly I recognized the ugly robin-blue house across the street, and in that split second the whole world snapped back into focus. Although I was a little unsure of my sanity, at least I knew exactly where I was: an intersection I had been at hundreds of times, only four blocks from my home.

Memories are landmarks that keep us from getting lost. They bring a sense of security and belonging to a child's life. They anchor deep in the soul and come back throughout life, reminding us of who we are and where we are. I like Edith Schaeffer's analogy of a museum. We do our kids a great service by filling their museum with a valuable collection of good memories.

Laugh Together

Diane and I and the two girls were camping deep in a remote Colorado wilderness when we stumbled upon an outdoor chapel. Years before, someone had discovered a pulpit-shaped rock, arranged several logs as pews, and made a beautiful little place that invited spontaneous worship. I stepped into the pulpit and suggested that we take a moment to thank God for the incredible beauty that surrounded us, but Taryn, about four years old at the time, interrupted my impromptu devotional. "I want to preach," she announced.

I surrendered the platform and joined Diane and Traci on the log pews. Taryn was wearing a red jacket with a pointed hood, and when she stood behind the rock pulpit all you could see were two eyes and the pointed hood. With a sweeping gesture, she began. "God made all this," she proclaimed, her squeaky little voice almost lost in the vast forest. "He made the trees, he made the rocks, he made the sky," she said, looking from side to side and gesturing toward everything she saw. "He made the squirrels, he made the leafs, he made this jacket." All we could see were the gestures, two eyes, and the hood. I tried to maintain some semblance of reverence, but Traci and

Diane lost control and began laughing uncontrollably. This brought silence from the preacher, who stepped out from behind the rock pulpit and impaled her sister with a self-righteous stare that could have killed a rattlesnake. "I learned all this from the Bible," she said. "But you don't even read the Bible. You don't even know how God made people," she scolded, shaking her finger at Traci.

Between gasps for air, Traci asked, "How did God create people, Taryn?"

Taryn was so serious and so authoritative as she homed in on her sinner sister. "First God took some mud," she proclaimed. "Then he scrunched it up like clay and made the mud into Adam." Taking a deep breath, she continued. "Then he saw that the man didn't have any friends. So God knocked Adam out, took out his lungs, and gave them to a woman."

I fell off the log.

At first, Taryn was angered by seeing us roll on the ground, but she quickly joined in our laughter. When we finally settled down, I praised her for her knowledge of creation and helped her straighten out some of the details. Even as I write this, the memory of those eyes and that hood sticking above the rock cause me to laugh out loud.

I have a wish for my funeral. I want my family to laugh. No, I don't want them dancing around the church, celebrating because I'm gone. But when the service is over and everyone is eating potato salad at the post-funeral feed, I hope my kids will be huddled in a corner, laughing until they're sick, remembering the good times. I pray that Traci will remember the hours we spent together in deserted parking lots as she learned to drive. I hope laughter will burst from her as she recalls how my head would snap back and forth as the car lurched across the lot. My neck still hurts at the very mention of a clutch.

I pray that Taryn will laugh as she remembers the family outing where she dumped a bucketful of crabs out the third-story window of a seaside condominium to set them free. Needless to say, they all died in the escape attempt. I hope she remembers the tears of laughter that came one day in Florida; just as I was about to speak to several hundred kids at a camp, she came running in the back door of the auditorium, out of breath. "Can an alligator run faster than a person?" she asked.

"Of course it can," I said. "Why do you ask?"

"Because," she declared, "me and my friend Labre are poking one in the eye with a stick." The camp kids had to wait while I accompanied my daughter to the back of the building to find a huge, angry alligator squinting through a very bloodshot eye.

Perhaps the blow of grief will be softened when they remember the great times we had with Togo, the most loving dog in the world. One day shortly after we brought Taryn home as a newborn, it became necessary to take her temperature. Three-year-old Traci watched with interest as Mom used the thermometer. Almost a week later, we were sitting in the dining room enjoying dessert with friends when we heard Togo begin to howl. We rushed into the kitchen to see Traci with the dog's tail in one hand and a yardstick in the other, determined to see if the dog had a fever.

One of the most difficult speaking assignments I ever had was in a part of the country where people are not given to showing their emotions. Ten minutes into my comedy concert entitled "A Reason for Joy," I was beginning to wonder whether these people had *any* reason for joy. The program was held in a large church, and the only thing echoing from the walls was an occasional cough. I unloaded the best comedy I had—routines that had never failed in the past. But the most I got was a chuckle from some of the braver souls in the audience.

I was particularly intimidated by an older gentleman sitting in the front row. His legs were crossed, his arms were folded across his chest, and the expression on his face was not unlike the one on Togo's face when Traci tried to take his temperature.

In twenty years of speaking, I had *never* received this kind of response. With sweat dripping from every pore in my body, I cut my program short and headed for the exit. The man with the Togo expression caught me halfway to the door.

"Young man," he said. (I braced myself for a lecture.) "That was the funniest program I ever saw. I thought I was going to die."

I wanted to say, *I thought you were already dead,* but was interrupted by his next comment: "It was all I could do to keep from laughing," he chuckled, a broad smile brightening his face.

I thanked the man and spent the night wondering why someone would try to keep from laughing at a comedy concert. What fun he missed. I was amazed again, a short time after that, as I talked with a group of high school kids, to discover that many of them rarely heard laughter in their home. Many of them were from loving homes, but the vital ingredients of fun and laughter were missing. Those valuable trophies would also be missing from their museum of memories.

Allow laughter to flood your home, and its echoes will last a lifetime. Someone wisely defined humor as a gentle way to acknowledge human frailty. I like to define it with the words I used in the first chapter of this book. Humor is a way of saying, "I'm not okay, and you're not okay, but that's okay. God loves us anyway." People who are secure in their awareness of God's love and who have experienced his loving forgiveness are free to laugh. Humor should never be used to avoid facing issues or as a weapon to hurt members of your family, but it should be allowed to flourish as a part of family life. Don't miss the fun of collecting memories of laughter for your kids' museum.

Play Together

One of the benefits of having kids is that it brings a new zest to living. During our children's early years of life, we spent enormous amounts of time simply enjoying them, playing with them, storing up memories for our own museums. Don't give in to the temptation to quit just because they grow older.

As we traveled across the country, my children had only one requirement for the hotel we stayed in: "Does it have a pool?" It didn't matter if roaches lay sunbathing around the pool's edges or leaves and debris lay at the bottom—if there was water, there was going to be fun. When they were young, I would always join them in the pool for safety's sake. (After all,

swimming takes on a new challenge when your one-year-old is making all the right motions and still drifting toward the bottom of the pool.) I would pretend to be a shark—a rare, finless species. I could send them screaming from the pool just by surfacing nearby and fixing them with my fishlike stare. One year I ballooned to 230 pounds and pretended I was "Orca the Killer Whale." That year the tidal wave I created just by jumping in would throw them from the pool. Some days I would pretend I was a beached whale, and they would spend many giggling minutes trying to drag me back into the water to save my life.

As they grew older, they still begged me to come and splash and play in the pool. But I declined because I had so much work to do, or because I was tired. In truth, I was too lazy. And it wasn't long before they stopped asking. It also wasn't long before they stopped swimming. After all, what fun is it to paddle around by yourself with no Dad to splash? What fun is it if you can't hold your parents underwater until their lips turn blue?

Don't stop playing with your kids. You are hanging portraits of love in their museums that will last forever.

I used to have my children collect items from all over the house and put them in a paper bag. Then I would sit down to read them a story. As I read, they were free at any moment to pull an object from the bag and hold it up. I was supposed to, without hesitation, incorporate that object into the story.

"Once upon a time there were three bears," I would read.

Out of the sack comes a toy car.

"Driving on the way to a Sunday school picnic," I ad-lib.

Out comes a pencil.

" 'Get the lead out,' mama bear said, as a driver slowed down in front of them." Giggles explode around me as I continue. "Little did they know that Goldilocks had entered their home and was sitting at their table. She tried the first bowl of porridge and wrinkled her face. 'This porridge is way too—'"

One of the girls whips out an old wig.

" 'Way too hairy.' "

Out comes a can of hair spray.

"If she had been wearing Final Net, this wouldn't have happened."

Lying on the floor in a heap of giggles, the girls would stop me and insist that it was *their* turn to tell a story while *I* pulled objects out of a bag.

Years later, my kids can't remember a single cartoon plot they saw on television back then. They can't even remember many of the gifts they got for Christmas. But their memories are rich with stories forever changed by the items in a paper bag. You don't need television, a mall, or a lot of spending money to have fun. A paper bag and a bunch of junk will do just fine.

Several years ago I gave up skiing. I got tired of eating snow during the day and having my bones whisper all night, "Give up skiing." But when both daughters fell in love with that diabolical sport, my heart overruled my bones. As kids grow older, the number of interests you have in common with them dwindles. If you don't make an effort to move in the direction of their interests, you may lose another important point of contact with your kids. Skiing with my daughters, I found, was made enjoyable simply because it gave me the chance to watch them develop skiing skills. But even more than that, I enjoy the fact that this sport helps us paint some priceless memory portraits together.

Create Tradition Together

When my daughters were younger, all I had to do was mention to them that we were going to be making a trip and they would immediately begin to ask, "Are we there yet? How much longer before we get there?" They would continue to ask those questions about every thirty seconds until we finally arrived at our destination. Just before their questions drove me over the brink, in a rare flash of genius I taught them to use the mileposts along the highway. After they'd learned to understand the mileposts, they always knew about how much longer before we would be there. All their anxiety disappeared.

If memories of laughter and fun are like familiar landmarks in an old neighborhood, then memories of tradition are like the mileposts on a highway. They have the power to soothe and heal, to take away some of the anxiety of life's journey.

In answer to the question "How can I begin to put a sense of togetherness into this harried household?" Dr. James Dobson wrote:

> Make a concerted effort to slow the pace at which your family is running. Beyond that advice, however, I would emphasize the importance of creating special traditions in your home. By traditions I'm referring to those recurring events and behaviors that are anticipated, especially by children, as times of closeness and fellowship between loved ones.[2]

Memories of tradition don't have to be humorous. Traditions are simply events that happen regularly, thereby giving shape to our lives—mileposts that enable your kids to look back to see how far they've come and to look forward in anticipation to what is coming. Family vacations, holidays, birthday celebrations, and the daily rituals of family life can all become traditions important to a secure childhood and a healthy adult life.

Planes, Trains, and Automobiles

Even as you've been reading this chapter, the faded memory of some wonderful little family tradition has probably come to your mind, and without knowing it you've been smiling. If you want your family vacation times to operate in that same way for your kids years from now, keep them simple, unhurried, and together. Do things that the whole family enjoys, and spend a lot of time doing nothing. How many times has a well-intentioned parent interrupted a structured, stressful vacation to announce to the kids, "You are going to enjoy this—*or else!*"

My daughters no longer enjoy camping—partly because there's no place to plug in a hair drier and because camping ruins newly polished nails, and partly because I didn't make it fun for them. Our camping trips were always combined with my hunting trips. The kids must have heard *Ssshhhh* hundreds of times.

"Daddy, look at the pretty flower!"

"Ssshhhh! You might scare a deer away."

I can remember on several occasions interrupting the most wonderful play at our remote campsites with, "Ssshhhh! You're making too much noise." How I wish I had taken the time to show interest in the things they enjoyed about camping. If I had, maybe they'd enjoy camping with me now.

It's not the complex and expensive things that last as memories—it's the simple things. V. Gilbert Beers observed:

> Ask your teen or older child about his most vivid and wonderful memory. You may be surprised at the answer. If you have been involved parents, that memory will likely focus on something you did with him. It will also likely be something you did unhurried, with no outside pressures. And it will likely be one of "the little things of life" rather than a five-star production. . . . I was surprised when we talked about a trip to Banff and Lake Louise. The Canadian Rockies are among the most magnificent mountains in the world. But the memories that jumped out first were: tiger ice-cream cones we bought in a little shop (black and orange ice cream swirled into a "tiger" pattern), a glass ball which reflected the mountains and lake, and a hike together along Lake Louise. They finally got around to the mountains as memories, but the mountains and scenery were up-staged by tiger ice-cream cones, a family hike, and an interesting glass ball.[3]

I grew up with very little tradition in my childhood, but the few little traditions we had stand out like beacons of warm light. After harvesting hay on a hot summer day, we would always drive about twenty miles to go swimming in Stony Lake. I've been gone from that place for almost thirty years; I can't remember the names of other rivers or lakes. I can't even remember many of the families that lived near us. But I remember Stony Lake. (There wasn't a stone within ten miles of that muddy little swimming hole.) There were no deep conversations. We didn't have a boat. We just relaxed together as a family. Every color, every smell, and every sound I can remember as though it were yesterday.

It was a tradition.

Birthday Cakes and Christmas Trees

Birthdays and holidays should stand out in a kid's mind like fireworks against a July sky—not because of expensive presents or elaborate trips, but because of the special traditions associated with those events.

Because birthdays were never a big deal in our family as I was growing up, I have to be very careful not to forget the birthdays of my family now. Sometimes I have to look at my driver's license to remember when my own birthday is. It shouldn't be that way. What better way to celebrate the worth of a family member than making that person king or queen for a day on the day they were born? On my fortieth birthday, my wife Diane surprised me with a houseful of friends and a marvelous party. Many of the guests gave tribute to our friendships and to my life.

I couldn't stop smiling for three days. That night as we prepared for bed I said, "Honey, every person on earth should have one day like this before they die."

To which she replied, "They ought to have a day like this at least once a year."

I agree. Hang some big, beautiful birthday memories in your kids' museum.

Every year at Christmas, two things stand out in our family. One is a trip we take to Grand Lake to be with dear friends; the other is a Christmas Eve ritual. When in Grand Lake, we do as the Grand Lakeans do—we share the traditions of our friends, which are different from our own. Our children have grown to love this wonderful change of pace and look forward to it every year. In our own Christmas Eve ritual, the girls produce and act in their own dramatic presentation of some aspect of the true meaning of Christmas. After that presentation, we declare our love for each other—each member of the family tells each other member one reason they love them. You may not believe this, but there's no hurry to open the presents. Yes, the girls are excited about the gifts they will receive, but their greatest excitement and anticipation is for our family traditions.

From Breakfast to Bedtime

Mealtimes and bedtime are two of the most sacred times in a family. Both have been attacked by the hectic schedules of twentieth-century living.

A teacher of several first-communion students was describing the Eucharist experience as a family gathering around a meal. She noticed students' eyes glazing over and realized she'd lost them.

Time for an illustrative question, she thought. "How often do you eat together as a family?" she asked her puzzled students.

She wasn't prepared for the scant show of hands. Fewer than half of them had regular family meals. A good number of them were in the habit of fixing their own meals and eating alone or with the television for company.[4]

If all you were able to do in your effort to establish some of the glue of tradition in your home was to take full advantage of these sacred moments, it would be enough. Your family table should be like the huddle of a football team—a place to discover the challenges and opportunities of each member of the team, and then to shout your encouragement to each other as you split up for another play; a place where ideas are shared and topics of interest discussed. Too often, because it is the only place we can (occasionally) get the whole family together, the table becomes a place of criticism and discipline. No wonder some kids seem to go out of their way to be away from the house at mealtime. Guard this time together as a family. These are mileposts you can't afford to lose. Work overtime to make mealtimes one of the positive memories in your home.

Bedtime, too, is sacred. I don't think there's another moment in the daily life of most children when they are so vulnerable to being loved and taught. This is one of the few times you can share uninterrupted moments with your child. From the time kids are small, they desperately attempt to prolong bedtime rituals. Taryn would yell religious questions from her room. "Daddy, does God talk to us?" she shouted one evening.

"Yes, he does," I responded from a couple of rooms away. "We'll discuss it in the morning."

"No," she shouted back. "We need to discuss it now, because God just talked to me." After a short, dramatic pause, she continued: "He said I could get up."

Taryn is now thirteen years old, and she still insists on being tucked into bed with a good hug and a goodnight kiss before she'll go to sleep. What a wonderful time to say "I love you." What a delightful way to end every day. What a perfect moment to thank God for his blessings and to seek his guidance for the coming day. Many adults have never forgotten the prayers their parents uttered at their bedside or the inspiration of Scripture read just before they went to sleep.

Clearly, bedtime is not the time for angry confrontation or discipline. It is the time to take advantage of your child's peaceful, receptive mind so that you can share expressions of inspiration, love, and encouragement.

Memories of Love

Not all of our important memories of childhood revolve around humor, birthdays, or vacations. Many of the adults I know treasure most the memory of a single moment that grew out of conflict resolution or parental forgiveness—a single moment in which, for the first time, they understood the enormous love of their mom or dad.

My friend Byron remembers the time he and his girlfriend had a minor accident that ruined his dad's new car. Fearful of what his father might say, Byron thought it might be wise to have his girlfriend with him when he broke the news. They got home very late. Byron knocked gently on his parents' bedroom door. Standing in the semidarkness with his girlfriend beside him, Byron said, "Mom and Dad, we have some bad news."

He had no idea how this must have looked to his parents until his mom tearfully exclaimed, "Oh *no*, Byron."

He quickly explained that the bad news had nothing to do with an unexpected pregnancy; rather, that he had just dented the brand-new car. At that, his father sat up straight in bed and questioned him thoroughly—but not about the condition of the car. That was never mentioned. Instead, his dad wanted to know about their own physical condition. His only concern was that they had not been hurt. Even so, Byron knew that his father was proud of that car, and finally he asked his dad what they were going to do about it.

"Cars can always be replaced," his dad responded. "You and your girlfriend can't."

Today, twenty years later, if you ask Byron about his father, you will hear that story. It is a memory that will last as long as he lives, a monument to the unconditional love of his father.

Someday, your children will be eating potato salad after bidding you their last goodbye. Let's hope that what they remember in those hours will be the legacy of love you left them. During that difficult time, they will tour their entire memory museum, looking for comfort and strength. They will count all the mileposts you provided for them to see how far they have come in their journey. What you are doing today will determine what they find there.

Ken Gire put it most beautifully in his moving tribute *A Father's Gift*:

A shiver of my own mortality runs through me.

What pictures will my son remember
 when he comes to the plain granite marker
 over his father's grave?
 What will my daughters remember?
 Or my wife?

What pictures will be left behind
 for them to thumb through
 in the nostalgic, late afternoons
 of their lives?

Will the pictures strengthen them for the journey?
 Or send them hobbling through life, crippled. . . .

I've resolved to give fewer lectures,
 to send fewer platitudes rolling their way,
 to give less criticism,
 to offer fewer opinions.

After all, where does it say that a father
 has to voice an opinion on everything?
 Or even have an opinion on everything?

From now on, I'll give them pictures they can live by,
  pictures that can comfort them,
  encourage them,
  and keep them warm in my absence.

Because when I'm gone, there will only be silence.
And memories.[5]

Positive memories are a source of strength that can serve as mileposts to help your children keep a healthy perspective on life as they grow to be adults. And the more positive memories you're able to put into your children's memory museum, the less powerful will be those memories of the times of conflict and difficulty that come to every family.

Someday, when your kids have grown to be adults, they will travel hundreds of miles to get together with other brothers and sisters or to visit you. Listen carefully to their conversation. If their museums are full, you will hear these words: "Remember when . . ."

NOTES

CHAPTER 1: I'm Not Okay, You're Not Okay, But That's Okay

1. Steven R. Covey, *The Seven Habits of Highly Effective People* (New York: Simon and Schuster, 1989), 18–19.
2. Ibid., 39.

CHAPTER 2: Looking for Trouble

1. Jay Kesler with Ron Beers, *Parents and Teenagers* (Wheaton, Illinois: Victor Books, 1984), 43.
2. Ibid., 27.

CHAPTER 3: No News Is Bad News

1. Ken Davis, *How to Live With Your Parents Without Losing Your Mind* (Grand Rapids, Michigan: Zondervan, 1988), 90.
2. H. Steven Glenn and Jane Nelsen, *Raising Self-Reliant Children in a Self-Indulgent World* (Rocklin, California: Prima Publishing, 1988), 90–91.
3. Ibid., 106, 112.

CHAPTER 4: Learning to Talk Gooder

1. Glenn and Nelsen, *Raising Self-Reliant Children*, 91.
2. Covey, *The Seven Habits*, 33.
3. Sherod Miller, Ph.D., Daniel Wackman, Ph.D., Elam Nunnally, Ph.D., and Carol Saline, *Straight Talk: A New Way to Get Close to Others by Saying What You Really Mean* (New York: NAL-Dutton, 1982), 251.

4. Dr. Ross Campbell, *How to Really Love Your Teenager* (Wheaton, Illinois: Victor Books, 1981), 60.
5. Ibid., 63.
6. Ibid., 67–68.
7. Ibid., 65.

CHAPTER 5: Discipline Is Not a Dirty Word
1. *The Merriam-Webster Dictionary Pocket Edition* (New York: Simon and Schuster, 1974).
2. James Dobson, *Dare to Discipline* (Wheaton, Illinois: Tyndale House, 1970), 9. All rights reserved.

CHAPTER 6: Walking the Tightrope
1. Josh McDowell and Dick Day, *How to Be a Hero to Your Kids* (Dallas: Word, 1991), 28.
2. Ibid., 37.

CHAPTER 7: Fertilizing Your Kids
1. *Fundamentalist Journal*, October 1984.
2. "American Teens Speak: Sex, Myth, TV, and Birth Control," The Planned Parenthood Poll, Louis Harris and Associates, Inc. (September/October 1986): 48. As quoted in *Josh McDowell Research Almanac and Statistical Digest*, 1990.

CHAPTER 8: The Talk
1. *People* (April 13, 1987): 116.
2. Family Research Council, "Trouble for Our Teens," *Washington Watch* 1, no. 4 (January 1990): 1. As quoted in *Josh McDowell Research Almanac and Statistical Digest*, 1990.
3. "American Teens Speak," 13.
4. Dr. Theresa L. Cremshaw, M.D., "Ten AIDS Myths Answered," *AIDS Protection* (September 1989): 3. As quoted in *Josh McDowell Research Almanac and Statistical Digest*, 1990.
5. Barry and Carol St. Clair, *Talking with Your Kids About Love, Sex and Dating* (San Bernardino: Here's Life Publishers, 1989), 47.
6. Phil Donahue, *The Human Animal* (New York: Simon and Schuster, 1985), 157–58.
7. *Rocky Mountain News* (August 28, 1991): 8.
8. Quoted in *I Don't Remember Dropping the Skunk, But I Do Remember Trying to Breathe* (Grand Rapids, Michigan: Zondervan, 1990), 121.

CHAPTER 10: What the World Needs Now
1. Alan Loy McGinnis, *The Friendship Factor* (Minneapolis: Augsburg, 1979), 87.

2. Zig Ziglar, *Raising Positive Kids in a Negative World* (New York: Ballantine, 1989).
3. Miller, Wackman, Nunnally, and Saline, *Straight Talk*, 249.
4. Josh McDowell, *How to Help Your Kids Say No to Sexual Pressure* (Dallas: Word, 1987), 19.
5. Barry and Carol St. Clair, *Talking with Your Kids*, 38.

CHAPTER 11: Working Yourself Out of a Job
1. Campbell, *How to Really Love Your Teenager*, 28.

CHAPTER 12: Remembering the Good Times
1. Edith Schaeffer, *What Is a Family?* (Old Tappan, New Jersey: Fleming H. Revell, 1975), 189–91.
2. James Dobson, *Dr. Dobson Answers Your Questions* (Wheaton, Illinois: Tyndale House, 1982). All rights reserved.
3. Jay Kesler, editor, *Parents and Teenagers* (Wheaton, Illinois: Victor Books, 1984), 266.
4. *Youthworker Update* (September 1990). Copyright Youth Specialties, Inc. Used by permission.
5. Ken Gire, *A Father's Gift* (Grand Rapids, Michigan: Zondervan, 1992), 52–53.

ABOUT THE AUTHOR

Ken Davis is one of the most sought-after speakers in North America. After fifteen years working in Youth for Christ, he has worked for the last fifteen years as a motivational and inspirational speaker. Ken provides a unique mixture of side-splitting humor and inspiration that never fails to delight and enrich audiences of all ages.

Ken has written five books, including *How to Live With Your Parents Without Losing Your Mind.* His books have received national critical acclaim, including the Campus Life "Book of the Year" award and the Gold Medallion award.

As president of Dynamic Communications, Ken provides seminars and a video series that teach speaking skills to ministry personnel and corporate executives. Born and raised in Minnesota, he is a graduate of Oak Hills Bible Institute. He and his wife, Diane, now live in Colorado with their daughters, Traci and Taryn.

Ken can be reached for speaking engagements by writing Dynamic Communications, 6080 W. 82nd Drive, Arvada, CO 80003, or by calling (303) 425-1319.